THE FIRST 100 YEARS

Regular Edition:
ISBN 10: 1-56037-567-1
ISBN 13: 978-1-56037-567-8

Special Edition:
ISBN 10: 1-56037-589-2
ISBN 13: 978-1-56037-589-0

Cover: Bear Lake. Photo by Erik Stensland.
Back flap: Author photo (top). Photo by Richard K. Young.
Back cover: Ranger at Chasm Lake. NPS photo courtesy of Rocky Mountain National Park Archives.
Map on page 4 by Deb Santos Schmaus.

For more information about our books, write Farcountry Press, P.O. Box 5630,
Helena, MT 59604; call (800) 821-3874; or visit www.farcountrypress.com.

Library of Congress Cataloging-in-Publication Data

Young, Mary Taylor, 1955-
  Rocky Mountain National Park : the first 100 years / by Mary Taylor
Young.
     pages cm
  ISBN-13: 978-1-56037-567-8
  ISBN-10: 1-56037-567-1
1. Rocky Mountain National Park (Colo.)--History. 2. Rocky Mountain
National Park (Colo.)--Biography. I. Title.
  F782.R59Y68 2014
  978.8'69--dc23
                              2013006706

Created, produced, and designed in the United States.
Printed in China.

18 17 16 15 14   1 2 3 4 5

Rocky Mountain National Park

THE FIRST 100 YEARS

By Mary Taylor Young

FARCOUNTRY
PRESS

Contents

For more than a century, people have come to Rocky's trails seeking "rest and hope," fulfilling Enos Mills' vision for the Park.
Photo by Erik Stensland.

Foreword

by Senator Mark Udall

THE STORY OF AMERICA'S NATIONAL PARKS, much like the story of the West, is an epic chronicle of exploration, ambition, and grandeur. And yet, for so many of us who call Colorado home, national parks—and the stories that take place in them—are deeply personal.

National parks not only provide unparalleled opportunities for hiking and mountaineering, but they also allow us to escape for weekend adventures with friends and teach environmental stewardship to our children. Throughout my time in Congress, preserving national parks has been one of my top legislative priorities, and in 2009, I sponsored a bill designating 250,000 acres of Rocky Mountain National Park as wilderness, the strongest protection the government can give to public lands.

Rocky Mountain National Park contains some of the most spectacular terrain in Colorado. Each year, millions of visitors marvel at the park's majestic peaks, sixty-four of which tower at over 12,000 feet. Gently sloping trails give way to craggy rock passes, as elk, moose, and deer meander among the aspen groves. The park's granite stones have witnessed thousands of years of human history as hunter-gatherers, miners, homesteaders, and ranchers passed through, some seeking refuge, others fortune. This history is humbling: We share this land, and we share in its protection.

At the dedication of Rocky Mountain National Park a century ago, the naturalist Enos Mills remarked, "In the years to come when I am asleep beneath the pines, thousands of families will find rest and hope in this park." Today the park is a testament to Mills' quiet vision. Each time I visit, I am awed by its magnificent landscapes, unique wildlife, and superlative recreational opportunities.

A bighorn sheep lamb poses near Rock Cut along Trail Ridge Road.

NPS photo by Russell Smith, courtesy of Rocky Mountain National Park Archives.

Acknowledgments

WHEN I BEGAN RESEARCHING THE HISTORY OF Rocky Mountain National Park, from its geologic beginnings billions of years ago to its future in the 21st century, I knew I was going to need help. I got that help, in spades, from many terrific people who shared their time, expertise, advice, research skills, personal histories, and friendship to help this book come into being. I am deeply indebted to all of you.

From the outset, Larry Frederick, now-retired Chief of Interpretation at Rocky, was enormously helpful and supportive of this project. He was my go-to guy when I needed to locate information, expertise, or get clarity on a Park issue. Thank you, Larry.

Thanks to Park superintendent Vaughn Baker, who gave me a sense of the big picture of Rocky's history, from pivot points in its first 100 years to insight on what challenges the future may hold. A great many Park employees shared their experience and professional knowledge to help make

this book accurate and timely: Gary Miller, Jeff Connors, Paul McLaughlin, Mary Kay Watry, Judy Visty, and Lindsay Colgrove of the natural resources staff; Kathy Brown, Leslie Brodhurst, Leanne Benton, Jeanne Muenchrath, Barbara Hoppe, Michele Simmons, Mark DeGregorio, and Kyle Patterson in interpretation, education, information, and public affairs; Sybil Barnes and Mariah Robertson for library and archive guidance; and Tim Burchett and Katy Sykes for great help in locating historic photos, some of which hadn't been published previously. Also thanks to Jim Detterline and Michael Smithson for sharing their stories and photos of their exploits.

I am also honored to have been a 2012 Artist-in-Residence (AIR) at Rocky Mountain National Park. I had the delight of living in the Park for two weeks at the historic William Allen White cabin (now forever known to me as "my cabin in Moraine Park"). To write about Rocky and its

history while actually living there was wonderful. Thanks to Jeanne Muenchrath and the AIR staff, and to the National Park Service for sponsoring the program.

Thanks also to Nancy Wilson and Rachel Balduzzi of the Rocky Mountain Nature Association for answering questions and sharing historic images. Janet Robertson was very helpful in sharing her insight and knowledge about Dr. Bettie Willard. Thanks to Dr. Bob Brunswig, Emeritus Professor of Anthropology at the University of Northern Colorado, for information on early human occupation of the Park and for sharing photography from his long-running archaeological survey. Thanks to Dr. Rob Benson, Professor of Geology and Earth Sciences at Adams State College, for his review of the chapter on Rocky Mountain geology.

Alicia Mittelman of the Estes Park Museum helped tremendously with locating historic photos and postcards. Thanks very much to Dave Lively

and Kathy Means of the Grand Lake Historical Society for sharing stories from the often overlooked west side of the Park, and for rounding up hundreds of historic photos. Dave Tanton generously shared his knowledge of Estes Park artists and his wonderful art collection. Jim Pickering, Estes Park historian extraordinaire, was very helpful with his meticulously researched books. Thanks to Phimister Proctor "Sandy" Church, grandson of the sculptor Alexander Phimister Proctor, for helping me understand the influence of the mountains on his grandfather's art.

Last, but very far from least, a huge thanks to my writing colleague and dear friend Cory LaBianca, who always welcomes me to her Estes Park home whenever I need a place to lay my weary head when I am in Estes, whether researching, writing, teaching, or just in need of a friend to share a glass of wine. This project would have been much harder (and a lot less fun) without you, Cory!

Introduction

"In its first 100 years, Rocky Mountain National Park achieved the proposed vision of being a premier national park. It is still remarkable that people at the beginning of the 20th century had the insight to ask Congress to set this Park aside. It was quite a gift to future generations."

— Vaughn Baker, Superintendent, Rocky Mountain National Park

IN 2015, ROCKY MOUNTAIN NATIONAL PARK celebrates 100 years as a national park. This book commemorates that milestone, attempting to capture in words and pictures a sense of the Park's grandeur and landscape, its rocks and mountains, its wildlife and unique plant community, and its people, both past and present.

Writing a book about a place with "Rocky Mountain" in its name must discuss geology and how mountains are formed, so this 100-year history really begins with the dawn of time. And, since any good history ends with a look ahead, it wraps up with some thoughts on the Park's future in the 21st century.

Over 100 years, Rocky Mountain National Park has changed in many ways. Glaciers have grown and receded, great lodges have been built and then removed. Management strategies have continually evolved, reflecting changes in the attitudes, knowledge, and awareness within American society. Human activity and environmental change continue to alter the landscape. But through decades of ebb and flow, Rocky Mountain National Park endures.

Rocky is a park with two faces. The high ridge of the Continental Divide bisects it north to south into an eastern side and a western side, each with its own distinct character.

Entered through the gateway town of Estes Park, the east side is drier, less forested, marked by numerous roads and hiking trails, and is, on average, higher in elevation. Easily accessible from the densely populated Front Range urban corridor, the east side has much higher visitation.

The lusher, wetter west side, accessed through the gateway town of Grand Lake, is home to the headwaters of the Colorado River. With only one main road and fewer trails and campsites, it offers a less-crowded feel for those getting off the road and out of the car.

Both sides of the Park are open year-round, but the alpine road that connects them is not. Trail Ridge Road is the highest continuous paved road in the United States, reaching an elevation of 12,183 feet. It generally opens in late May and stays open through mid-October, depending upon snowfall. In the months the road is open, visitors drive through spectacular scenery, climbing from open valleys upward through forests that change in character with elevation.

At its highest point, Trail Ridge Road carries visitors through a land that few people would likely ever see otherwise—the alpine tundra. This austere, open landscape, where only the hardiest plants and animals survive, is Rocky's crown jewel. It encompasses one-third of the Park's 415 square miles. In this land above the trees, wrote author Ann Zwinger, "the sky is the size of forever and the flowers the size of a millisecond." The Park's extensive alpine ecosystem led to its designation in the 1970s as the Rocky Mountain Biogeographic Province by the United Nations.

The Park preserves some of the most rugged and spectacular scenery in the Rocky Mountains. It offers a bastion where visitors can discover silence, find spiritual renewal, and connect with nature. Hundreds of elk gathered in the Park's open valleys give visitors a rare glimpse of long-ago North America, when vast congregations of wildlife once roamed. Those who venture away from roads on lesser-traveled trails can experience an hour, or a day, when they neither see nor hear another human, only the natural sights and sounds of the mountains.

A rich human history is found in the Park, from traces of ice age hunters to the remnants of 19th-century ranches and homesteads. Rocky is also a park that particularly reflects America in the 20th century. As the country fell in love with the automobile, this Park came into its own. Just sixty miles from a major metropolitan area, it has always been an auto-touring park, attracting large numbers of locals as well as destination visitors from throughout the nation (and the world). When Americans hit the road to see their national parks in the family car, Rocky welcomed them, taking them deep into its rugged wilderness to discover the heart of the mountains, and the grandeur of America. It is a park that leaves a lifelong impression on many who visit in their youth.

Alpine avens brighten a slope below Longs Peak.
NPS photo courtesy of Rocky Mountain National Park Archives.

Congress established Rocky Mountain National Park on January 26, 1915, as the nation's tenth national park. It predates the 1916 creation of the agency that administers it, the National Park Service. Rocky encompasses approximately 265,800 acres, or 415 square miles. It protects stunning mountain scenery, including Longs Peak, a "fourteener" that rises to an elevation of 14,259 feet and is climbed by thousands of visitors a year. The Park is home to hundreds of species of native plants and wildlife. Visitors might glimpse moose, beaver, and coyotes, and discover native wildflowers with names like fairy slipper and elephant head. Ninety-five percent of the Park is designated wilderness. It has 359 miles of trails, 150 lakes, 476 miles of streams, and 113 peaks that rise more than 10,000 feet in elevation.

No wonder more than 3 million people visit each year, making Rocky the fifth most visited national park in the country.

The foresight of those who preserved this special place, and all national parks, for future generations is remarkable. They knew it was imperative to protect the mountains and wilderness then, not later. Without their vision and hard work, what Americans know today as Rocky Mountain National Park would be dotted with private homes, hotels, gas stations, and neon signs. Because of the foresight of these early conservationists, we have Rocky Mountain National Park, one of the great treasures of the National Park System.

The Park's rugged landscape tells a geologic story rich in drama and surprises.
Photo by Erik Stensland.

A Story of Mountains

A REMARKABLE STORY LIES BENEATH *the majestic peaks and rich valleys of Rocky Mountain National Park. It is the tale of a turbulent past, of immense powers that shaped the land, raised giants and brought them low, then raised new ones in their place.*

If geologic time could be speeded up, the formation of Rocky Mountain National Park would play out in a grand spectacle. Crashing tectonic plates, mountains thrusting upward miles into the air, seas flooding the land and then receding. Spouting volcanoes, flows of lava, fields of ash. Rivers of ice locking the land in a cold embrace, carving the faces of mountain peaks, gouging out valleys, directing rivers, piling great mountains of debris. The shape and form and composition of the land changed again and again.

Other national parks preserve stunning mountain beauty, but it is Rocky Mountain National Park that best showcases its namesake mountains. Though the rocks that make up these magnificent peaks are billions of years old, the mountain range itself is "new"— if something millions of years old can be called that. Mountain ranges rose and fell repeatedly in Colorado over a billion years. The current Rocky Mountains, the "new" ones, did not uplift until between 70 and 40 million years ago.

Rock Making

The rocks that comprise the Park's highest mountains, rising more than two miles above sea level, once lay at the bottom of the sea. Their formation began nearly 2 billion years ago, during the Precambrian, when sediments built up in ancient seas. Molten rock solidified to form the Earth's crust, made up of numerous pieces called tectonic plates that move, shift, and push against each other. Intense heat and pressure from the collision of the plates eventually converted these sea sediments into schist and gneiss, types of metamorphic rock. Marked with sparkling

The south wall above Chasm Lake reveals alternating layers of granite and schist, the building blocks of many of the Park's mountains.
Photo by W. T. Lee, July 23, 1916, courtesy of U.S. Geological Survey.

Rocky's rocks tell stories of uplift, glaciation, and erosion.

NPS photo by John Marino, courtesy of Rocky Mountain National Park Archives.

flecks of black mica, these are the oldest rocks in the Park, estimated to be more than 1.5 billion years old. The uplift of mountains that was to come would raise these sediments nearly ten miles from where they formed on the sea bottom.

Magma, or molten rock from within the Earth, intruded through this metamorphic rock. The magma eventually cooled to form a massive intrusion of granite, which makes up the bedrock of most of the mountains in the Park. Called Silver Plume granite, it is a grainy rock made of feldspar, quartz, and mica, and colored pink, white, and gray. The 1,000-foot, sheer-faced cliff on Longs Peak known as The Diamond is composed of this ancient rock, which is sometimes referred to as Longs Peak granite. At Rock Cut along Trail Ridge Road, thin streaks of pinkish Silver Plume granite are visible as intrusions into the surrounding dark, sparkly schist.

Molten rock again intruded the Precambrian crust about 1.3 billion years ago, forming the ridge-like Iron Dike. This formation of dark igneous rock known as gabbro, extends at least sixty-eight miles from south of Boulder far into Rocky Mountain National Park. Outcrops of the Iron Dike are visible north of Trail Ridge Road near Mount Chapin and at Hidden Valley.

Over millions of years, the Precambrian sediments were further buried within the Earth, but they wouldn't stay there. Three hundred million years ago, a mountain range rose in what is now the Park. These were not the Rocky Mountains we know today, but the Ancestral Rockies. Over millions of years, water scrubbed away at these mountains, dissolving and washing away a layer of rock nearly two miles thick, until the land was leveled down to a rolling plain. Where did the eroded sedimentary rock go? It forms the Fountain Formation, a 1,200-foot-thick layer of sandstone along the eastern edge of the Front Range of the Rockies. The dramatic Flatirons in Boulder, Red Rocks in Denver, and Garden of the Gods in Colorado Springs are exposed outcrops of the Fountain Formation.

By 140 million years ago, the Park was once again covered by water. The vast, inland Cretaceous Sea stretched from Mexico to Canada. The climate was warm, varying from semi-arid to tropical or subtropical. The sea's shoreline, and the landscape, constantly shifted, resulting in swamps, lakes, and coastal dunes. Instead of the pine trees of today's Park, there were dense thickets of ferns and cycads. Giants roamed the land. Countless bones and tracks found in sedimentary rocks in the Rockies tell of dinosaurs and other animals that inhabited the area during the Jurassic and Cretaceous periods.

But something was happening deep underground. Always in motion, the tectonic plates that comprise the Earth's crust began to collide along what was then the western edge of North America. As these two massive landforms pushed against each other, something had to give.

The Birth of Mountains

Orogeny. It means the birth of mountains. Beginning about 70 million years ago, the collision of two monsters, the Pacific and North American tectonic plates, caused a great folding uplift in the area that is now the western United States. The Pacific plate subducted, or slid underneath, the North American plate, eventually reaching as far as Wyoming, Colorado, and New Mexico. The enormous heat and pressure caused the Earth's crust to crack and buckle. Colossal blocks of ancient metamorphic rock, topped by layers of sedimentary rock, were thrust upward. Before this great uplift, the rocks that are now at the top of Longs Peak

*The face of
The Diamond
on Longs Peak
spans nearly
1,000 vertical feet.*
NPS photo courtesy of Rocky
Mountain National Park Archives.

lay some 13,000 feet below the surface. This period of mountain birth is known as the Laramide Orogeny. It was during this time of geologic upheaval that the present-day Rocky Mountains were born.

A mountain range can't rise up without a tremendous ripple effect, and as the land lifted, the Cretaceous Sea retreated, exposing the thick sediments that had built up on the sea bottom. With the land rising upward, water naturally flowed downward, forming streams and rivers. Over time, the exposed sea sediments eroded away until the ancient Precambrian rocks—the schist and gneiss with their intrusions of granite—were again uncovered. Erosion worked on them as well, scrubbing away until the landscape was again gently rolling. The rounded slopes atop Trail Ridge and Flattop Mountain are remnants of this scoured landscape.

But the geologic forces of the Earth are continually at work, and the Rocky Mountains would not remain a series of rolling hills. About 10 million years ago, the Earth's crust pushed up again, heaving skyward

*Formed along a
geologic fault, Longs
Peak continues to rise.
The Diamond and
Mills Moraine as
viewed from the
top of Twin Sisters.*
Photo by W. T. Lee, June 19, 1916,
courtesy of U.S. Geological Survey.

Longs Peak

At 14,259 feet, Longs Peak is the only "fourteener" (a mountain rising to an altitude of 14,000 feet or more) in Rocky Mountain National Park. It is also the Park's highest point. The peak's distinctive, boxy top and flat summit are visible far to the east on the Colorado prairie.

This "new" mountain is made of "old" rock. While its core is part of a massive intrusion of Silver Plume (also called Longs Peak) granite formed more than a billion years ago, its present shape was sculpted much later by glaciers. At one time, rivers of ice flowed down Longs Peak on all sides. The

The cirque in the East Face of Longs Peak is known as The Chasm, cradling Chasm Lake. The sheer East Face rises about 2,400 feet above the lake.
Photo by W. T. Lee, July 22, 1916, courtesy of U.S. Geological Survey.

glaciers retreated and advanced over millennia as the climate warmed and cooled and warmed again, gradually chiseling the peak into its present, familiar profile. The Diamond—the dramatic rock wall on the East Face of Longs that is a popular climb for mountaineers—is a 1,000-foot granite cliff offering a glimpse into the rocky makeup of the peak. This sheer rock face, and the other vertical cliffs that form Longs' box-shaped summit, are the headwalls of ancient, glacier-carved cirques—large, bowl-shaped amphitheaters surrounded on three sides by cliffs. Water collecting in the cirque below The Diamond feeds Chasm Lake, a classic tarn or mountain lake.

The spectacular landscape of chasms, cliffs, and tortured ridges spreading out from the summit of Longs Peak across the Park's highest country owes its drama to the creative forces of ice.

more than a mile. Like a hot-air balloon expanding slowly to full height, an enormous dome, including all of Colorado and parts of Kansas and Utah, lifted the Earth's crust. Longs Peak and some other mountains rose even higher along fault lines. Even today, the mountains continue to rise.

Volcano!

Stresses from the formation of the Rocky Mountains pulled apart the Earth's crust in what is now the Park's west side. Granitic magma rose through these deep faults, pushing the crust upward to form volcanoes in the present area of the Never Summer Mountains. This range of mountains is younger and of different origin than the other mountains in the Park. Their tops originally stood several thousand feet higher than the present peaks.

Between 29 and 24 million years ago, the volcanoes erupted, spewing ash and lava. Specimen Mountain is one of these extinct volcanoes. Though its crater was erased by erosion, its sides are made of volcanic glass, lava, ash, and pumice stone. The Lava Cliffs along Trail Ridge Road also formed during this period, when a massive flow of volcanic ash and pumice solidified. High above the east side of the Kawuneeche Valley, a rock feature made of volcanic rhyolite remains as evidence that ash and lava flowing from one of the Never Summer volcanoes at one time filled the valley. Water and glacial erosion over millions of years sanded away most of the volcanic rocks and re-carved a valley, leaving just this remnant of rhyolite.

Over time, the towering volcanoes of the Never Summer Mountains eroded down to their present size and shape. But their steeper slopes and jagged profiles compared to the Park's other peaks, and their arrangement in a north-south line, remain as evidence of their volcanic heritage.

Layers of pumice, lava, and ash form the flanks of 12,489-foot Specimen Mountain, revealing its volcanic origin. This breccia outcrop, worn by erosion, contains blocks of lava and boulders of schist and granite.
Photo by W. T. Lee, August 1902, courtesy of U.S. Geological Survey.

The peaks of the Never Summer Range are old, eroded volcanoes, in contrast to the uplifted and glaciated mountains of Rocky's Continental Divide ranges.
Photo by W. T. Lee, August 23, 1916, courtesy of U.S. Geological Survey.

Rivers of Ice

The great forces of the Earth formed the rocks and lifted the mountains of Rocky Mountain National Park, but it is the action of glaciers, much later in time, that shaped and carved much of its magnificent scenery, like a sculptor chiseling and chipping away at marble.

Glaciers form from the compaction of snow year after year into a mass of ice. While they look solid and immobile, glaciers are actually in motion. Pulled downhill by the force of gravity, they move like immensely slow rivers. As they advance, they scrape away the land, re-forming the V-shaped valleys carved by streams into wider U-shaped valleys. A glacier carries along soil and rocks, depositing it in piles of debris called moraines. Material deposited to the sides of a valley as a glacier advances forms lateral moraines. Material pushed ahead of a glacier and deposited when the glacier stops advancing forms a terminal moraine, a ridge at the foot of a valley like a pile of dirt pushed up by a bulldozer.

The first major glaciation in the Park took place 1.6 to 2 million years ago. Then the Earth's climate warmed and the glaciers receded. The ice returned between 300,000 and 130,000 years ago, again locking the land beneath a cold blanket. This second glaciation left isolated moraines at various places in the Park.

Once again the climate warmed, the ice released the land, and it was 100,000 years until the third glacial episode. The Pinedale Glaciation began some 30,000 years ago during what is popularly known as "the Ice Age." At its zenith about 21,000 years ago, most of the Park's valleys were filled with ice up to 1,500 feet thick. If visitors had stood along what is now Trail Ridge Road, they would have seen a glacier thirteen miles long filling Forest Canyon. On the Park's west side, instead of the scenic Kawuneeche Valley, with lush green meadows alongside the meandering oxbows of the Colorado River, they would have viewed a glacier twenty miles long!

When the climate once again warmed, between

From the foot of Round Top Mountain, the view west toward Grand Lake encompasses a vast glacial valley. The valley's rounded ridges, carved and polished by repeated glaciation, are known as roche moutonnees, *or* sheepbacks.
Photo by W. H. Jackson, 1874, courtesy of U.S. Geological Survey.

15,000 and 12,000 years ago, the massive glaciers melted away. But the evidence they left behind is in plain sight today. A half mile beyond the Fall River Entrance Station, the highway climbs a terminal moraine left by the final advance of a glacier. That glacier scraped the U-shaped valley of Horseshoe Park, leaving sandy soil and piles of boulders as evidence of its passage. Lateral moraines nearly 1,000 feet high rise on three sides of the aptly named Moraine Park. As visitors drive the Bear Lake Road from the Beaver Meadows Entrance Station to Moraine Park, they travel up and over a lateral moraine. The Moraine Park Visitor Center sits on the terminal moraine of this glacier-carved valley. Continuing to Bear Lake, visitors travel along and over the South Lateral Moraine, then along the Bierstadt Moraine. On the west side, the enormous glacier that filled the Kawuneeche Valley left a lateral moraine that helps retain the waters of Grand Lake, a natural lake filling a glacier-carved basin.

Along Trail Ridge Road, the immense artistry of glaciers is showcased in the incredible vistas of cirques, lakes, moraines, and horseshoe-shaped valleys. These carved and sculpted landscape features lie in stark contrast to the rolling, unglaciated ridges and open terrain of the tundra.

The Continental Divide

When visitors travel from one side of Rocky Mountain National Park to the other over Trail Ridge Road, they pass over the Continental Divide. But what does that mean? The Rocky Mountains rise like a spine, running the length of western North America from north to south. Water flows one direction on the east side—to the Gulf of Mexico and the Atlantic Ocean—and another direction on the west side—to the Pacific Ocean. This ridge of mountains literally divides the continent of North America into its two main watersheds. Hence, the Continental Divide!

The Divide, however, is not the highest landscape in the Rockies. Peaks rise higher than the Divide on both sides of it. Longs Peak, the highest point in the Park, lies east of the Continental Divide. Its waters flow ultimately to the Atlantic Ocean.

In this aerial view, the Bierstadt Moraine is clearly visible as the ridge running in a gentle "S" through the middle of the frame. The Bierstadt is a lateral moraine, formed along the side of a glacier's path.
NPS photo courtesy of Rocky Mountain National Park Archives.

Millennia ago, the Mills Glacier on the east flank of Longs Peak carved an immense gorge and a small cirque lake, as seen from the Keyhole.

Photo by W. T. Lee, July 24, 1916, courtesy of U.S. Geological Survey.

Are There Still Glaciers in
Rocky Mountain National Park?

The Rocky Mountain Nature Association published this guide to glaciers within Rocky in 1959.
Photo courtesy of Rocky Mountain Nature Association.

Visitors often mistake perennial snowfields for glaciers. These masses of snow that persist through the summer do not move significantly, while glaciers can be thought of as rivers of ice, flowing slowly downhill.

Andrews, Tyndall, and Rowe glaciers are the last true glaciers in the Park. (Tyndall Glacier is a half mile long and is large enough to have an ice cave within.) Known as cirque glaciers, they are found in bowl-shaped depressions (cirques) at the head of valleys where snow tends to accumulate and there is little direct sunlight that would hasten melting. Cirque glaciers are remnants of much larger glaciers that once filled the Park's valleys. There are also numerous rock glaciers in the Park. Like ice glaciers, these masses of rock with ice frozen in the spaces between them flow downslope. All the Park's glaciers are on the east side where snow blowing over the mountains from the wetter west side continually adds to their icy bulk.

In historic times, Rocky's glaciers have never been the vast ice rivers of ancient times, but they have fluctuated in size. During the first half of the 20th century, they retreated, meaning they melted at a faster rate than snow accumulated. A warming climate shrank the glaciers to their smallest recorded size in the mid-1940s. Cooler summer temperatures advanced the glaciers through the 1980s, but since the 1990s, hot summers have shrunk most of the Park's glaciers to historic minimums. The effects of the current global warming trend may eventually melt away Rocky's glaciers and snowfields.

Wearing crampons for traction, a survey crew maps Andrews Glacier in the cirque south of Otis Peak, 1966.
NPS photo courtesy of Rocky Mountain National Park Archives.

The old Ute Trail crosses
boulder-strewn alpine terrain.
Photo by Glenn Randall.

2

Early People of the Park

Frost tinged the air, *but the hunters, huddled with their spears beneath animal skins in the shallow pits, sweated nervously. They listened for the shouts of their kinspeople and the drumming hooves of the animals being driven toward them. The elk they waited to ambush weighed as much as 900 pounds and could easily trample a man to death.*

Above them, on the barren alpine tundra of what in 5,000 years would be Rocky Mountain National Park, two low walls of rock spread away from them in a widening funnel. Somewhere across the tundra, the women, children, and older people of the band were waving hides, whooping, and driving a group of elk ahead of them toward the funnel's wide mouth. And toward the hidden hunters. The success of this autumn hunt meant survival for the people through the coming winter. The price might be the life of one or more of the hunters.

Today, the only evidence of such long-ago hunts are the remains of low rock walls, stacked to form ingenious traps known as game drives. All of the eight prehistoric game drives discovered in the Park are on the tundra. The drives were probably in use for at least 9,000 years, based on radiocarbon analysis of Paleo-Indian projectile points found at nearly all the game drives in the Park. Native Americans abandoned the use of game drives by the early 1800s, after they acquired horses. This technological advance allowed them to switch from the slow herding of elk and bighorn sheep into traps to the rapid chase and killing of game from horseback.

A paleolithic-era game drive wall remains visible on the tundra in Rocky Mountain National Park.
NPS photo courtesy of Rocky Mountain National Park Archives.

Paleolithic hunters placed rocks to form a game drive wall on Mount Ida.

Photo by Jack Moomaw, 1937, courtesy of Rocky Mountain National Park Archives.

Ice Age People

It's easy to look at the uncluttered vistas and lack of buildings in Rocky Mountain National Park and think the area is a preserved wilderness untouched by humans prior to the arrival of Euro-Americans in the 1800s. But evidence of people in the Park dates back at least 11,000 years, when ice age hunters, known as Paleo-Indians, began migrating through the area with the retreat of the glaciers.

The wide, rolling landscape of Rocky's tundra creates a natural passage across the Continental Divide, for both animals and humans. For thousands of years, nomadic bands followed the movements of animals across the aptly named Trail Ridge. As their game migrated onto the high tundra in late summer with the greening of the grass and alpine plants, the people followed. They made camp within the shelter of trees at timberline, where they left abundant evidence—small flakes from toolmaking or sharpening, rock ring hearths, stone tepee rings, spear points and

arrowheads, stone knives, and scrapers. All the ancient campsites found by archaeologists have artifacts that date back over 9,000 years.

On the tundra above their campsites, they stacked rocks to make game drives. These ancient hunters also gathered roots, berries, and food plants and processed meat for later use. Grinding surfaces known as metates, and hand-held grinding rocks called manos—used to pound meat, berries, and fat into pemmican—have been found at high altitude.

Archaeologists have found some 400 prehistoric sites within the Park, with evidence of many different prehistoric cultures, including Clovis, Folsom, Archaic, and Ceramic periods.

Ice age wanderers crossed the Park's high country to the plains to hunt mammoths and other now-extinct species. Their descendants followed the same routes in later centuries to hunt bison on the Colorado prairie. Native Americans visited the Park's valleys, forests, and high peaks through the warm months of

The Return of the Arapahos

As youths, Arapaho elders Gun Griswold and Sherman Sage had ridden, fought the Utes, and hunted across the vistas of Rocky Mountain National Park. They returned in 1914. Members of the Colorado Mountain Club, working to build support for the establishment of the national park, invited the two Arapaho elders on a horse pack trip through the area to share the Indian names for many landscape features. By that time, Griswold was seventy-three, a solemn, retired tribal judge who spoke no English. Sixty-three-year-old Sage, who was chief of the Arapaho tribal police on the Wind River Reservation in Wyoming, was more loquacious—as jolly as Griswold was quiet. They were accompanied by Tom Crispin, an Arapaho interpreter. Led by white guide Shep Husted, the group spent two weeks riding through what would soon be a national park, telling stories and sharing the Arapaho names for mountains, lakes, streams, and rock formations. Longs Peak and Mount Meeker were known together as "The Two Guides," Griswold and Sage remembered, because seen from the plains of northern Colorado, they are a prominent landmark and appear to be a double peak. Volunteer Oliver Toll, then twenty-two, recorded extensive notes, though he waited nearly fifty years to publish them as a book—*Arapaho Names and Trails*. Thanks to that historic visit, thirty-six place names within the Park are of Arapaho origin, including Kawuneeche Valley on the west side of the Park. *Kawuneeche* is the Arapaho word for coyote. Lumpy Ridge, Never Summer Mountains, and Big Meadows are also translations of Arapaho place names. Many of those Arapaho words may themselves be translations of the original Ute names.

In 1914, several prominent Arapaho elders visited Estes Park and the area soon to become Rocky Mountain National Park. From left to right: (standing) Shep Husted, Gun Griswold, Sherman Sage, Tom Crispin, Oliver Toll, and (seated) David Hawkins.
NPS photo courtesy of Rocky Mountain National Park Archives.

the year to hunt elk, deer, and bighorn sheep. They gathered lodgepoles for tepees and performed sacred rituals. Arrangements of rocks in distinctive ways suggest native people came to the Park seeking spiritual guidance. Some sacred features were recognized by contemporary Ute elders as what their people used historically, such as stone prayer rings and crescent-shaped walls for vision quests. More than thirty sacred sites associated with spiritual activities have been identified. By analyzing lichens growing on the rocks, archaeologists have dated some to be as much as 1,100 years old.

Native people also left abundant pottery fragments, some of it made by "the locals," such as the

A Ute war party on horseback, 1899.
Photo by H. S. Swartley, courtesy of Denver Public Library.

Utes' Uncompahgre brownware, while others likely came through trade. Potsherds found along Forest Canyon Pass in the 1940s were made by the Apaches. Other pottery came from the Shoshone in Wyoming.

People of the High Mountains

In historic times, the Utes and Arapahos were the primary tribes using the area of the Park, but these two peoples were (and still are) very different. The Utes inhabited the Park seasonally for at least 900 years, the Arapahos for about 75. The Utes are culturally a Great Basin tribe; the Arapahos are Plains Indians. The Utes came to the Park from the western

mountains. The Arapahos arrived from the eastern prairies. The Utes speak a Uto-Aztecan dialect, while Arapaho is in the Algonquian language family. Whether because of their differences, or the simple fact that they competed for territory and food, the two tribes became implacable enemies.

For centuries, the Utes were the dominant people of the Colorado mountains. They spent winter in the relatively mild intermountain valleys of western Colorado, moving into the high mountains in summer to hunt, fish, and gather seeds and roots. Their ancestors likely inhabited the area of the Park for 6,000 years. The Utes were composed of seven bands

Ute Chief Sevara poses with his family, circa 1885.
Photo courtesy of History Colorado (Scan # 20103577).

Ute Chief Ignacio with his horse, circa 1904.
Photo by Frank S. Balster, courtesy of Library of Congress (LC-USZ62-112572).

Runs Medicine, an Arapaho, holds a shield and tomahawk, circa 1899.
Photo courtesy of Library of Congress (LC-USZ62-101281).

A wickiup's simple construction belied its effectiveness at providing shelter from harsh weather.
NPS photo courtesy of Rocky Mountain National Park Archives.

Old Man Gun's Eagle Trap on Longs Peak

The Arapaho medicine man crouched in a pit atop the highest peak. The bird of prey he waited to trap, a bald eagle, had two-inch-long, razor-sharp talons. The medicine man had to be patient, stealthy, and, when the time came, lightning fast, for an eagle is no animal to take lightly.

On his 1914 trip through the Park, seventy-three-year-old Gun Griswold shared the story of an eagle trap his father, Old Man Gun, had built long ago atop Longs Peak. Old Man Gun excavated a hole at the summit, its entry just big enough for him to squeeze through. The space below was just big enough for him to sit in. On the rocks above, visible to an aerial hunter, he placed a stuffed coyote carcass and some tallow as bait. Then he settled in his hiding place to wait.

Iconic Longs Peak figures in ancient tribal lore as richly as in contemporary climbing history.
NPS photo courtesy of Rocky Mountain National Park Archives.

Spotting the stuffed coyote from a great distance, a soaring eagle swooped in to investigate. When it landed by the decoy, Old Man Gun reached up from below the coyote decoy and grabbed the eagle by the legs. The talons of an eagle are fearsome and his grab had to be quick and true.

Old Man Gun used some kind of herb spread on his hands, said Griswold, so that as soon as he touched the eagle, it would have a fit and become helpless. It was a secret herb that he also used to catch the wildest horses in the country.

The Longs Peak eagle trap? No one has found evidence of it on the summit, but then, it was a long time ago.

that at one time lived throughout central and western Colorado and eastern Utah. The Grand River, Yampa, and possibly the Uncompahgre bands made use of the Park, probably first entering the area in the 1200s. In the early 1600s, the Utes came into contact for the first time with Europeans—Spanish explorers and settlers. The Spanish brought with them a technology that would transform Ute life—horses.

Utes were Great Basin hunter-gatherers who lived in brush wickiups. They trapped small game, taking larger game when they could, dug roots and bulbs, and foraged other plants for food. When they acquired horses, the Utes adopted the lifestyle of Plains Indians, including their dress, tepees, and the efficient bison hunt. With horses to transport things, the Utes' material culture increased and they ranged over a wide area, including across the Continental Divide to the plains to hunt bison.

In contrast with the Utes, the Arapahos were Colorado newcomers. How and why they came to live on the Great Plains is unclear. They were probably at one time semi-settled agricultural people from Minnesota and North Dakota, who were pushed gradually westward by attacking tribes such as the Cree and Assiniboine. Arriving on the Colorado prairie in the late 1700s and living in close association with the Cheyenne, they also adopted a nomadic, Plains Indian lifestyle—inhabiting tepees and hunting bison on horseback. The Arapahos probably never numbered more than about 2,500 people. In summer, they ventured into the mountains to hunt. There they came into conflict with the mountain people, the Utes.

The Utes resented incursions into their territory, and unceasing hostilities began between them and the Arapaho and Cheyenne tribes. One story tells of a

Apache Fort

The peaceful valleys and quiet forests of the Park seem unlikely battlefields, but many fights took place here among the Utes, Arapahos, and other tribes. A collection of boulders on a rock outcrop at the upper end of Beaver Meadows is said to be the remains of a defensive fort built by a war party of Apaches as they made their last stand in an epic battle.

A visitor points to the rock formation known as Apache Fort.
NPS photo courtesy of Rocky Mountain National Park Archives.

According to a story told by Sherman Sage, the Arapaho elder who visited the area in 1914, his people fought the battle with Apaches in the early 1850s, when he was four years old. He remembered the wounded, including his oldest brother, being brought into camp. This was a major battle, according to Sage, and became a part of the oral history of the tribe.

The Arapahos met the Apache war party of about fifty men in Beaver Meadows and a pitched battle followed. For more than a day the Apaches made a stand at a spot Sage called Apache Fort. He said it was a ring of stones that the besieged Apaches piled up along the edge of the rocky cliffs as a defensive fortification. Eventually the Arapaho chief ordered his warriors to allow the surviving Apaches to escape to the north.

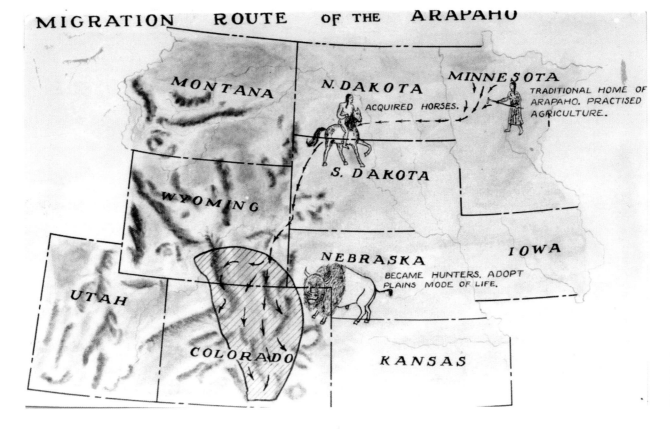

A map showing the presumed migration route of the Arapaho.
NPS photo courtesy of Rocky Mountain National Park Archives.

raiding party of the two tribes' warriors that followed the Ute Trail, along what is now Trail Ridge Road, over the Continental Divide to attack a band of Utes camping at Grand Lake. For protection during the fight, the Ute women and children floated out onto the lake on hastily made rafts. The Ute warriors defeated their attackers, but their triumph was fleeting. During the battle, the fragile rafts broke apart and their families tragically drowned.

By the time American settlers arrived in the area, the free-roaming life of the Arapahos and Utes was waning. Joel Estes and his family, who built the first cabin in the Estes Valley in 1860, never saw Indians. "There were signs that Indians had been there at some time, however," wrote Joel's son Milton in his memoir, "for we found lodge poles in two different places. How long before, we could not determine."

The Utes still hunted in the Kawuneeche Valley in the 1860s and 1870s. But by the 1870s, treaties had restricted the territory of both the Arapahos and the Utes, and they were eventually removed to reservations outside of Colorado by the U.S. government. Occasionally hunters left the reservations to prowl the mountains and valleys in the area as late as the 1890s. Consolidated into the Northern Ute tribe, the three Ute bands that once inhabited the Park now live on the Uintah and Ouray Reservation in northeastern Utah. The Northern Arapahos live on the Wind River Reservation in Wyoming, and the Southern Arapahos live in Oklahoma. Three Ute bands living in southwestern Colorado clung to their corner of the state and avoided removal. Today they inhabit the Southern Ute and Ute Mountain Ute reservations, the only Indian reservations in the state.

The Native Americans who once hunted and traveled the Park left abundant evidence behind—arrowheads, tepee rings, pottery fragments, branch wickiups (conical structures used as temporary shelter), cleared areas, and arrangements of stones that may have been sites of vision quests. Their heritage lives on in the names of the valleys and mountains where they once lived.

Mountain majesty and a sparkling river—the Big Thompson—make Moraine Park a highlight of any visit to Rocky.

NPS photo by Ann Schonlau, courtesy of Rocky Mountain National Park Archives.

An Arapaho tepee once stood as part of an Arapaho Indian History exhibit at the museum in the Moraine Park Visitor Center, date unknown.
NPS photo courtesy of Rocky Mountain National Park Archives.

The Old Ute Trail

The alpine terrain of Rocky Mountain National Park has long been a byway, a passage across the Continental Divide from the central mountains to the Eastern Plains. For generations, people on foot, and later on horseback, wore a well-defined route into the tundra that is still in evidence today—the Ute Trail. Eleven-thousand-year-old Clovis projectile points discovered on the trail indicate its use since prehistoric times. The Arapahos referred to it as The Trail Where Children Walk because portions were so steep young children had to get off the horse-drawn travois so that the horses could make it up the incline. Trail Ridge Road follows part of the Ute Trail, and hikers willing to brave mercurial weather, exposure, and thin air can cross the mountains along two portions of the trail—from Upper Beaver Meadows to Trail Ridge Road on the east, and from Milner Pass to the Alpine Visitor Center on the west—just as mountain people have done for millennia.

The Ute Trail climbs above Forest Canyon —and the clouds.
NPS photo by John Marino, courtesy of Rocky Mountain National Park Archives.

Snowmelt sluices down from Mount Dunraven in the Mummy Range.
Photo by Erik Stensland.

3

Early Exploration and Settlement

"*W*E STOOD ON THE MOUNTAIN *looking down at the headwaters of the Little Thompson Creek, where the Park spread out before us. No words can describe our surprise, wonder and joy at beholding such an unexpected sight. It looked like a low valley with a silver streak or thread winding its way through the tall grass, down through the valley and disappearing around a hill among the pine trees. This silver thread was Big Thompson Creek. It was a grand sight and a great surprise.*"

— Milton Estes, "Memoirs of Estes Park," *Colorado Magazine,* July 1939

A New People Comes to the Park

The sudden, stunning view of Estes Valley, with its backdrop of dramatic peaks, has delighted many visitors since Milton Estes and his father, Joel, first viewed the valley in October 1859. Joel Estes was among the hordes of prospectors attracted to the Rocky Mountains during the Colorado Gold Rush. He and nineteen-year-old Milton rode into the mountains along an Indian trail to hunt and prospect. At the sight of the valley's lush grass, rushing streams, and abundant wildlife, Joel's thoughts turned from gold to the money he might make ranching. The next year, father and son drove cattle up the rugged trail and built the first cabins in the valley that would bear their name. The site of that first ranch, near the present-day intersection of U.S. Highway 36 and Fish Creek Road, is now beneath the waters of Lake Estes.

Native Americans had lived here seasonally for thousands of years, and the area was also probably known to trappers, mountain men, and adventurers. The first written account of the area came from wanderer Rufus B. Sage, who wrote of his September 1843 ramblings through what is now Estes Park and the eastern side of the national park, "a concentration of beautiful lateral valleys, intersected by

In 1858, a year before arriving in the valley that would bear his name, Milton Estes carved his name into Register Cliff, near Guernsey, Wyoming.
NPS photo courtesy of Rocky Mountain National Park Archives.

With Longs Peak in the background, the Big Thompson River threads through an untrammeled Estes Park in this image from the 1873 Hayden Survey.
Photo by W. H. Jackson, courtesy of U.S. Geological Survey.

Joel Estes, here with his wife, Patsey, left Kentucky to prospect for gold in California, Oregon, and then Colorado. He and his son Milton first laid eyes on the valley that would bear their name in the fall of 1859. They built a homestead there in 1860, but the climate proved too harsh for cattle ranching, so they sold out and left in the spring of 1866.
Photo courtesy of History Colorado (Scan # 10029518).

Seen here from the summit of Twin Sisters, the valley of Estes Park retained much of its undeveloped character until well after the establishment of Rocky Mountain National Park.
Photo by W. T. Lee, July 1916, courtesy of U.S. Geological Survey.

meandering watercourses, ridged by lofty ledges of precipitous rock, and hemmed in upon the west by vast piles of mountains climbing beyond the clouds . . . ."

In 1863, Joel Estes brought his wife and younger children to live in the valley. Milton Estes, who had married in 1861, brought his wife, Mary, and their two sons to the valley. Mary bore a third son, Charles, in 1865, the first white child born in the area.

It was a lonely and isolated life, but in 1864 the Estes family hosted visitors, launching the valley's first tourism. *Rocky Mountain News* founder and editor William Byers and a party arrived to climb Longs Peak and stayed at the Estes ranch. They failed to reach the summit, leading Byers to boldly pronounce in the *Rocky Mountain News,* "We are quite sure that no living creature, unless it had wings to fly, was ever upon its summit, and we believe we run no risk in predicting that no man ever will be." (Byers would later prove himself wrong.) In his newspaper accounts, he christened the valley "Estes Park."

William Newton Byers, founder and editor of Denver's Rocky Mountain News, *was among the climbing party to make the first documented ascent of Longs Peak in 1868.*
Photo courtesy of Denver Public Library.

The Highest Peak

In 1820, the Stephen H. Long expedition, charged with exploring western lands between the Mississippi River and the Rocky Mountains, made the first written record of the landscape that would become Rocky Mountain National Park—a sighting of Longs Peak from miles out on the Eastern Plains. The explorers mistakenly thought it "the point designated by Pike as the Highest Peak," that is, Pikes Peak, the dominant mountain noted by the Zebulon Pike expedition in 1806. Long's party did not enter the Park (though they did climb Pikes Peak a few weeks later). Their "highest peak" was named for the expedition's commander a few years later. Mount Evans, at 14,265 feet (6 feet higher than Longs) is actually the highest peak along Colorado's Front Range.

Early visitors admire The Diamond below Longs Peak's summit.
NPS photo courtesy of Rocky Mountain National Park Archives.

Visible far out on the plains, and dominating the landscape around Estes Park, Longs Peak quickly became an irresistible magnet for climbers. Native Americans undoubtedly climbed the peak, but the first recorded ascent was made in 1868. Renowned Colorado River explorer John Wesley Powell, scouting the headwaters of the Colorado, saw the peak and determined to climb it. His climbing group, which included *Rocky Mountain News* editor William Byers on his second attempt,

Rising to an elevation of 14,259 feet above sea level, and about 9,000 feet above the Eastern Plains, Longs Peak is one of the most prominent mountains along the Front Range.
NPS photo courtesy of Rocky Mountain National Park Archives.

approached the peak from Grand Lake. Their arduous route took four days. They traversed two 13,000-foot peaks that included many false summits. But eventually, on the morning of August 23, the group stood atop the summit of Longs Peak. They spent about three hours on top, taking measurements and looking for signs of previous human presence, which they didn't find. The group wrote their names on a piece of paper, which they put in a baking powder tin and wedged between the rocks—the first summit register on Longs Peak.

Word of this towering peak in the wilds of the American West had already reached Europe. In 1865, French novelist Jules Verne used it as the site of a fictional observatory with a 280-foot-long telescope in his book *From the Earth to the Moon*.

How High Are Them Thar Hills?

After the Civil War, the U.S. government dispatched various expeditions to map western lands, triangulate the elevation of mountains, find the headwaters of major rivers, describe landforms, and draw, describe, and collect the strange flora and fauna of the American West.

The U.S. Geological and Geographical Survey of the Territories, better known as the Hayden Survey after its leader Ferdinand Vandeveer Hayden, surveyed in Colorado from 1873 to 1875. It measured and named many peaks within the future Park, including Mount Meeker and Mount Lady Washington. A party that included Hayden, *Rocky Mountain News* editor William Byers, and celebrity mountaineer Anna Dickinson climbed Longs Peak on September 13, 1873. They triangulated the height of Longs Peak at 14,271 feet, only 12 feet off from the currently accepted elevation. More newsworthy at the time was Miss Dickinson's ascent, thought to be the first by a woman. Even more earthshaking was that she climbed the mountain dressed scandalously in trousers.

Renowned photographer William Henry Jackson accompanied the Hayden expedition, capturing dozens of images on fragile glass photograph plates. His outstanding pictures of the vistas, peaks, and valleys of the future national park record a wild mountain landscape as yet little-changed by human action.

Ferdinand V. Hayden (1829–1887) was a physician and geologist with a talent for exploring wide swaths of the American frontier. In later life he taught geology at the University of Pennsylvania in Philadelphia and also served as a geologist for the U.S. Geological Survey.
Photo circa 1880, courtesy of U.S. Geological Survey.

William Henry Jackson (1843–1942) was a painter, illustrator, publisher, Civil War veteran, and explorer, but he is perhaps most famous for his more than 80,000 photographs of the early American West. Jackson also served as a technical advisor for the movie version of Gone with the Wind.
Photo circa 1880, courtesy of U.S. Geological Survey.

Roughing it on the Hayden Survey didn't necessarily preclude sit-down dinners. Ferdinand Hayden is seated first on the left.
NPS photo courtesy of Rocky Mountain National Park Archives.

A few abandoned log buildings still stand as markers of Lulu City along the headwaters of the Colorado River.
NPS photo courtesy of Rocky Mountain National Park Archives.

The small cabins typically erected by early prospectors and trappers provided cramped living quarters, but also critical shelter from the mountains' harsh elements.
NPS photo courtesy of Rocky Mountain National Park Archives.

Winters were severe in the mountains, and despite the lush grass, raising cattle for profit was hard. In 1866, Joel Estes sold the ranch, reputedly for a single yoke of oxen. The land passed through several more owners until purchased by Welshman Griffith J. Evans in 1867.

Settling the West Side

While the Estes family was pioneering a life on the east side of the Divide, fur trapper Philip Cranshaw built the first cabin on the west side, near Grand Lake, in 1857 or 1858. He stayed in the area until 1861, trapping beaver and other animals along the North Fork of the Colorado River and trading them for the gold that other men were digging out of the ground. In 1867, Joseph Westcott arrived, built a cabin at Grand Lake, and nearly froze to death his first winter. He stayed on, hunting, fishing, trapping, and occasionally prospecting, even writing an epic poem, *The Legend of Grand Lake*. This longtime resident became the first postmaster of Grand Lake and one of the area's most picturesque pioneers.

Hope of quick riches from gold and silver discoveries drew others into the mountains. A short-lived mining boom on the west side along the Colorado River gave birth to the town of Lulu City and nearby mining camps, Dutchtown and Gaskill, which boomed and busted in the early 1880s.

Lulu's Ghost

On the west side of the Park, a popular hiking trail leads to a genuine Colorado ghost town. Lulu City was born during a short-lived mining boom near the headwaters of the Colorado River. In 1880, speculators William Baker and Benjamin Franklin Burnett platted a 160-acre townsite and named it for Burnett's beautiful daughter. At its peak, Lulu City boasted 500 residents as well as sawmills, groceries, general stores, saloons, and even a dairy with twenty cows imported all the way from Denver. Miners' tents and new cabins dotted the slopes as men dug into the mountains in a desperate search for quick riches. But in the classic boom-and-bust cycle typical of Colorado's mining history, hopes for a fortune in gold or silver quickly played out. The ore produced by area mines was low-grade, not worth the cost to transport it down the mountain to a mill. By the end of 1883, the boom was over. All that remains today of Lulu City are the rotting remnants of a few log buildings.

An old flume leads to remnants of a sawmill in Lulu City.
NPS photo courtesy of Rocky Mountain National Park Archives.

Fear of Indians kept many white settlers out of the mountains, but by 1880, with removal of the Utes and Arapahos to reservations by the federal government, ranches and homesteads blossomed on both sides of the future Park. In the last decades of the 19th century and first part of the 20th, many settlers, including some whose names live on in landmarks within the national park, tried their hand at ranching and farming.

Euro-Americans began moving to the east side of the future park. Griff Evans raised cattle on the former Estes ranch. Homesteader and future lodge owner Abner Sprague took up residence in Moraine Park. Reverend Elkanah Lamb settled at the foot of Longs Peak, which he climbed, and guided others up, many times. His precipitous descent of the mountain on one near-fatal trip is memorialized in the name of the chute he tumbled down—Lamb's Slide. Elkanah's cousin, Enos Mills, who would campaign diligently in later years for establishment of Rocky Mountain National Park, joined him on the homestead in 1884 at the age of fourteen. Wealthy English aristocrat, the Earl of Dunraven, began buying up land in the Estes Valley.

The more remote west side was slower to be settled. Miner Joe Shipler stayed on after the demise of Lulu City in 1883. The remnants of his cabins are still visible along the Lulu City Trail. In the 1890s, the Harbison sisters homesteaded adjacent parcels of land and operated a dairy farm in the Kawuneeche Valley. In 1900, after serving in the Spanish-American War, "Squeaky Bob" Wheeler began ranching 160 acres on the west side of Milner Pass. Around 1917, the Holzwarth family homesteaded along the Colorado River.

But the high altitude, hard winters, unpredictable weather, rugged terrain, and long distance to market made earning a living by ranching a difficult proposition. Increasingly, adventurers, climbers, and sightseers showed up at the remote ranches asking for a meal and a place to stay. Guests, area settlers began to realize, were a lot less work than cattle. And they paid in cash.

A new industry—tourism—had arrived.

Judging from this 1906 photograph, "city" was an optimistic sobriquet to bestow on Lulu City.
Photo courtesy of Grand Lake Historical Society.

Born in 1831, the eldest daughter of an English clergyman, Isabella Bird traveled the world, writing a dozen popular books on the people and natural histories of the United States, Hawaii, Japan, China, Korea, and Africa. Bird was the first woman admitted to the Royal Geographical Society.
Photo courtesy of History Colorado (Scan # 10026773).

The Lady and the Ruffian

One of the earliest "celebrities" to visit the area was globe-trotting Englishwoman Isabella Bird. The genteel, forty-two-year-old Bird arrived in Estes Park in September 1873 to witness for herself the beauties of the mountains. She rented a cabin from Griff Evans, who owned the ranch established by Joel Estes, becoming one of the Park's first tourists. "Never, nowhere, have I seen anything to equal the view into Estes Park," she wrote, quite a statement considering she had just visited Hawaii. "The mountain fever seized me, and, giving my tireless horse one encouraging word, he dashed at full gallop over a mile of smooth sward at delirious speed."

Bird fell in love with the magnificence around her, and with the dominating aspect of Longs Peak, which she determined to climb. Though dissuaded by her host from attempting an ascent so late in the season, she found a willing ally in "Mountain Jim" Nugent. A colorful character, part gentleman and part ruffian, the one-eyed Nugent had been mauled by a grizzly bear, leaving one side of his face horribly disfigured, while the unmarred side, wrote Bird, was "strikingly handsome." She proceeded to be completely charmed by the courtly mountain man. "His manner was that of a chivalrous gentleman," she wrote, though "Desperado was written in large letters all over him . . . . A man any

woman could love, but no sane woman would marry."

Bird's account of their Longs Peak ascent is a lively read in her classic *A Lady's Life in the Rocky Mountains,* the story of her 1873 journeys through Colorado, which is still in print. Dressed in her "Hawaiian costume" and borrowed boots, Bird struggled to make the rugged climb in the thin air. Mountain Jim stayed by her side, pulling, pushing, prodding, and half-carrying the exhausted Bird to the summit. She fell repeatedly, so Nugent tied her to him by a rope, dragging her upward "like a bale of goods" and sometimes tugging until her arms "were half pulled out of their sockets." In steep stretches, he made steps for her with his hands or had her climb on his shoulders. Though she wanted to turn back, "Mr. Nugent," as she scrupulously called him, refused to let her give up. After a long and arduous climb, they stood upon the summit "in the splendour of the sinking sun, all color deepening, all peaks glorifying, all shadows purpling, all peril past."

Since her book was first published in 1879, the idea of a romance between the English lady and the courtly ruffian has fascinated readers. Though offered the princely sum of $6 a week by Griff Evans to stay on for the winter and do the cooking, Bird left Estes Park in late October, never to see Mountain Jim again. He was shot and killed less than a year later by Evans, in circumstances that are still mysterious. Whether or not the Englishwoman and the mountain man were in love will never be known, but their autumn idyll on the slopes of Longs Peak is memorialized in the name of Jim's Grove, their timberline campsite where he romanced her with stories and song.

The illustrated title page of the 1910 edition of A Lady's Life in the Rocky Mountains *depicts Isabella Bird in her riding clothes.*
Photo by Mary Taylor Young.

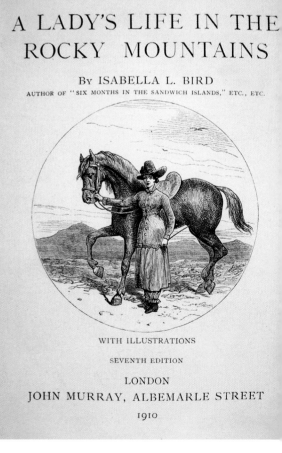

A LADY'S LIFE IN THE ROCKY MOUNTAINS

BY ISABELLA L. BIRD
AUTHOR OF "SIX MONTHS IN THE SANDWICH ISLANDS," ETC., ETC.

WITH ILLUSTRATIONS

SEVENTH EDITION

LONDON
JOHN MURRAY, ALBEMARLE STREET
1910

The Earl's Land Grab

In 1872, Windham Thomas Wyndham-Quin, the Fourth Earl of Dunraven, came to the Estes Park area on a hunting trip. Awed by the scenery and the vast amount of game—"Everything is huge and stupendous," he wrote—he determined to acquire the valley as his own private hunting preserve. Enlisting fellow Englishman Theodore Whyte as his agent and manager, he founded the Estes Park Company and began acquiring title to the land any way he could. This included enlisting drifters and unemployed cowboys to stake 160-acre claims under the Homestead Act, then buying the land from them for as little as $50.

Mountain Jim Nugent, who in 1873 guided Isabella Bird up Longs Peak, fiercely opposed the earl and his shady land grab. Nugent's land in Muggins Gulch occupied the primary access route into Estes Park, which may have led to his ultimately fatal encounter with Griff Evans. The Welshman Evans had sold his 1,000 acres to Lord Dunraven, and Nugent accused him of collusion. The men clashed, and Evans shot Nugent. Mountain Jim lingered nearly three months before succumbing. The earl, on hearing of Nugent's death, reportedly commented that it was a pity Evans hadn't shot the man sooner.

By 1880, Lord Dunraven owned 8,200 acres and controlled another 7,000. But his scheming property acquisition did not sit well with many locals. Many of the original homestead claims purchased by the earl's company had not been improved, as required by law, and some of the homestead filers had never visited the land before selling out. Reverend Elkanah Lamb chided those who dealt with the earl for being willing "to sell their souls for a mess of pottage." Meanwhile, other settlers claimed properties in the Estes Valley that had been overlooked by the earl's company. They built cabins and put up fences, pockmarking what the earl and Whyte had intended to be a vast private preserve.

Things got nastier as Theodore Whyte, like the evil ranch foreman in a Hollywood western, tried to force out small landholders who wouldn't sell. He ordered them off their own property, tore down fences, and drove the earl's cattle onto their land to graze. When Lord Dunraven's cowboys herded 200 head of cattle onto Abner Sprague's Moraine Park homestead, Sprague waited until they rode off, then rounded the cows up with his herd dogs and sent the cattle stampeding back to the earl's ranch, where they reportedly arrived before Whyte and his men.

Like most area settlers, Lord Dunraven could not exist solely on cattle ranching. In 1877, he got into the tourist business and built what was, for the area, a luxury resort. Locals called the Estes Park Hotel "the English Hotel." Even with tourism revenue, a cattle operation, and a sawmill, Lord Dunraven's Estes Park Company had difficulty making a profit. It faced a huge tax bill for the thousands of acres of land it owned. Lord Dunraven himself quit coming to Estes Park after 1881 and began selling off his property. By 1907, the last of the Earl of Dunraven's land was purchased by F. O. Stanley and his partner, who soon built the landmark Stanley Hotel. The future of Estes Park lay in tourism, not ownership by a single, wealthy landowner.

The earl's land grab had failed.

The Earl of Dunraven's land grab in Estes Park won him few friends.
Photo courtesy of History Colorado (Scan # 10026882).

When in Estes Park, the Earl of Dunraven lived in this home built in 1877 along Fish Creek.
Photo courtesy of Denver Public Library.

Dream Lake lies buried beneath a forty-four-inch April snowfall.
Photo by Glenn Randall.

4

The Rise of Tourism

ONE SUNNY DAY IN 1880, *a group of hikers appeared at the door of Abner Sprague's cabin in Moraine Park. They were exploring up the Big Thompson River, they told Abner and his mother. Would the homesteaders prepare a chicken dinner for the hikers to eat on their return in mid-afternoon?*

The proposition was a gamble for the Spragues. Money was hard to come by, but so were chickens. What if they killed several of their precious birds, but the hikers, wandering in the mountain wilderness, took a different route back and never showed up for their meal?

The Spragues agreed to feed the men. They killed and cooked several chickens, then waited, fingers crossed. The hikers did return, enjoyed a freshly cooked dinner, and paid handsomely.

It was then, Abner Sprague later wrote, with those chicken-dinner coins jingling in his pocket, that he realized it was easier to make a living in the mountains by milking tourists rather than milking cows.

A New Industry for the Mountains

Tourism quickly became the primary industry on both sides of the Park. Almost the moment Joel Estes finished building the first cabin in the area, he found himself in the tourism business when, in 1864, *Rocky Mountain News* editor William Byers and his Longs Peak climbing party stopped and asked for food and a place to spend the night before tackling the mountain.

The east side of the Park is only about sixty-five miles from Denver. As word got out about the area's scenic beauty, travelers increasingly arrived at area ranches and farms seeking lodging and meals. The dramatic edifice of Longs Peak, visible from far out on the prairie, drew climbers to the Park like moths to flame. In just a few decades, accommodations catering to tourists and climbers sprang up all over the meadows, forests, and mountains on both sides of the Continental Divide.

Much like today, early visitors were drawn to the mountains for the astonishing views and the exhilaration of climbing among the peaks. An intrepid group ascends Tyndall Glacier between Flattop Mountain and Hallett Peak.
NPS photo courtesy of Rocky Mountain National Park Archives.

The Estes Park Hotel featured banks of windows and a wrap-around porch overlooking a pond along Fish Creek with views of Longs Peak beyond.
Photo by W. H. Jackson, circa 1880, courtesy of Denver Public Library.

The first true hotel in the area was the Earl of Dunraven's Estes Park Hotel, built along Fish Creek in 1877. Known locally as the English Hotel, the three-story structure was a grand contrast to the rustic cabins dotting the valley. Its wide balconies, large windows, card and billiards rooms, artificial lake, golf course, and tennis courts attracted upper-crust clientele. But eventually the earl grew weary of fierce local opposition to his attempt to buy up and control the entire valley, and he sold his hotel and much of his land to F. O. Stanley. As was often the case with wood structures in an era when fireplaces were the source of heat, his English Hotel was destroyed by fire in 1911.

By 1880, the James family turned their ranch along Fall River into the Elkhorn Lodge. "Every summer people came to the ranch and begged to be allowed to stay," daughter Eleanor James Hondius later wrote,

"and each winter another cabin would be built on the ranch to house them." The Elkhorn became the largest resort in the area and is still in operation.

In the Shadow of Longs Peak

In 1875, the Reverend Elkanah Lamb, a United Brethren minister, built a cabin in the Tahosa Valley between Longs Peak and the Twin Sisters. Climbers were especially drawn to Lamb's ranch at the base of Longs Peak, and by 1880, the reverend was in the tourism business. He dubbed his rustic lodge Longs Peak House, and he and his son, Carlyle, did a steady business hosting climbers at the hotel and guiding them up the mountain.

In 1902 the Lambs sold out to Elkanah's young cousin, Enos Mills. Four years after purchasing the lodge, the original log building burned to the ground.

In his early days, Enos Mills lived in this small, rustic cabin, which he built himself.
Photo courtesy of Grand Lake Historical Society.

In 1908, Enos Mills built Timberline Cabin to offer food and lodging for climbers on the Longs Peak Trail.
Photo by W. T. Lee, July, 1916, courtesy of U.S. Geological Survey.

Undaunted, Mills rebuilt, using fire-killed trees to construct a much grander structure, which he dubbed Longs Peak Inn. Rustic and natural were still the bywords, however, and Mills offered visitors not only guided climbs of Longs Peak but nature walks and evening lectures. He forbade the picking of wildflowers. Dancing, smoking, drinking, and card-playing were likewise frowned upon. There was a limit to what privations tourists would tolerate, however, so Mills added steam heat in 1911 and electricity in 1916. To provide food and lodging for climbers, he built Timberline Cabin beside Longs Peak Trail in 1908.

Getting into the hospitality business gave the naturalist a greater stake in preserving the natural values of the Park. Since the Estes Park hotel season was limited to summer, Mills used the off-season to write articles and books and to lobby for the creation of Rocky Mountain National Park. His widow continued to operate the hotel after his death in 1922, but fire again took the main building in the 1940s. All that remains of the inn from Enos' day is a single building known as the Forest House, owned now by the Salvation Army.

Mr. Stanley and His Hotel

At the end of the 19th century, F. O. Stanley, the brilliant inventor and successful businessman, along with his twin brother F. E., made a fortune developing a dry emulsion for photographic plates. Even more high-profile, the brothers developed a steam-powered automobile, the Stanley Steamer, that was the fastest vehicle in the world at the time. But in 1903, when F. O. was fifty-four years old, his doctors gave him grim advice. Don't make plans more than a few months into the future. He was dying of tuberculosis.

Seeking a more healthful climate, Stanley visited Estes Park. Miraculously, his health improved. Determined to build a resort in the mountains, he partnered with Greeley businessman B. D. Sanborn to purchase Lord Dunraven's 6,400-acre estate, plus the Estes Park Hotel and other property, for $80,000.

Stanley envisioned a luxury resort where well-heeled patrons could enjoy the beautiful and restorative environs of the mountains without sacrificing their comfort. The five-story Stanley Hotel, which opened in 1909, featured 150 rooms in the central

At the turn of the 20th century, the town of Estes Park was little more than a cluster of wood-frame buildings lining a dirt main street and two side streets.
Photo by Robert Marshall, 1912, courtesy of U.S. Geological Survey.

With his twin brother Francis Edgar, Freelan Oscar Stanley invented and engineered the Stanley Steamer, America's most popular car in the early 1900s. Their initial fortune was built not on automobiles, however, but a photographic process, which they sold to George Eastman, founder of Kodak. Shown here in 1939 at age ninety, Stanley was an energetic promoter of the national park.
NPS photo courtesy of Rocky Mountain National Park Archives.

building, a 600-seat theater, basement bowling alley, laundry, ice house, golf course, employees' quarters, a carriage house with garage and machine shop, a smaller, adjacent Manor House for winter guests, and, in later years, its own airfield. The all-electric hotel was powered by a hydroelectric plant Stanley built to harness energy from the nearby Fall River.

Stanley transported his elite clientele from train stations in Longmont, Lyons, and Loveland via eleven-passenger Stanley Steamer transports, chugging them up the Big Thompson and North St. Vrain canyons along roads whose construction he helped finance.

Stanley didn't stop there. He became a major civic benefactor for Estes Park, organizing a bank, selling electricity to residents from his hydroelectric plant, donating property for parks and schools, and supporting the establishment of Rocky Mountain National Park. Over the years he earned the nickname "Grand Old Man of Estes Park."

What about the death sentence from tuberculosis that F. O.'s doctor had pronounced? It didn't happen.

Guests at the Stanley Hotel enjoyed grand views of Estes Park, with Longs Peak dominating the southwest horizon.
Photo by W. T. Lee, August 1916, courtesy of U.S. Geological Survey.

The Grand Old Man of Estes Park shares his porch with a Steller's jay.
Photo courtesy of Estes Park Museum.

Abner Sprague: Homesteader, Innkeeper, Park Pioneer

The young Abner Sprague was as industrious as he was dapper, building a three-story hotel and damming and enlarging a natural lake to create thirteen-acre Sprague Lake, a popular fishing and picnic spot to this day.
NPS photo courtesy of Rocky Mountain National Park Archives.

Abner Sprague first arrived in the Estes Valley in 1868. "I cannot describe . . . my feelings when I looked down on that tree-dotted flat and saw the stream winding through the unfenced meadow, the dark forest of the black canyon at the farther side and the snowcapped peaks topping all, cutting clear silhouettes in the deep blue of the sky." He fell in love with the place and homesteaded, along with members of his family, in Moraine Park, which he called Willow Park. But the Sprague's simple log cabin with the peat roof was inadequate for guests. Inspired by that chicken dinner and visions of paying guests, Abner Sprague and his family built a three-story hotel catering to middle-class visitors in the late 1880s. The high prices at Lord Dunraven's Estes Park Hotel, he reasoned, opened up an opportunity for a moderate-priced lodging house. He and his wife, Alberta, operated their hotel until selling out in 1904 to partner J. D. Stead and moving to a lower elevation.

Over succeeding decades, what was now Stead's Ranch and Hotel expanded across the grassy landscape of Moraine Park into a major resort complex that included guest cottages, a swimming pool, golf course, trout pond, stable and corrals, and numerous other outbuildings. Edgar Stopher, Alberta's nephew, bought the property in 1950. But upkeep of the mountain resort was expensive, so in 1962, Stopher sold out to the National Park Service, which was buying private inholdings within the national park. The structures were torn down and fencing and other evidence of settlement obliterated. Today, a seemingly untouched mountain valley greets visitors, offering little clue to the extensive development that once filled Moraine Park.

Alberta (left, seated on rock) and Abner (on horseback) Sprague pose for a family portrait with Sprague Ranch in the background.
NPS photo courtesy of Rocky Mountain National Park Archives.

For Abner and Alberta Sprague, the mountains never stopped calling. They moved back to the area and in 1910 opened a new hotel in Glacier Basin—Sprague's Lodge, which operated until 1958. The industrious couple dammed Sprague Lake and gave their name to many other features in the Park, including Sprague Mountain, Sprague Pass, Sprague Glacier, and Alberta Falls. Abner and his brother Fred laid out many Park trails that are still used today, including paths to Flattop Mountain, Loch Vale, and Mills Lake, and named many landscape features such as Fern Lake, Forest Canyon, Sky Pond, and Trail Ridge.

Abner Sprague is said to have bought the first paid entrance—$1, which was good for a year—to Rocky Mountain National Park in 1939 (entrance had been free until then). But in his memoir, longtime-ranger Jack Moomaw claimed Sprague's purchase was staged as a publicity stunt and that Moomaw had sold the real first paid entry to a tourist from Iowa.

Sprague lived in the area for nearly seven decades, noting with pride that he made his first ascent of Longs Peak on July 24, 1874, and his last exactly fifty years later on July 24, 1924, at the age of seventy-four. Such strenuous efforts must have been good for his health. Sprague lived almost another two decades, passing away in 1943.

Sprague eventually sold his Moraine Park homestead and three-story hotel to his partner, J. D. Stead.

Photo courtesy of Denver Public Library.

Abner Sprague enjoyed a long, robust life among the mountains and wildlife in Moraine Park. He passed away in Denver at age ninety-three.

NPS photo courtesy of Rocky Mountain National Park Archives.

Estes Park's "Grand Old Man" operated his hotel for two decades, finally selling it in 1929. Whether it was the beneficial mountain climate or some other healing influence, F. O. Stanley lived to the age of ninety-one. He died in 1940.

Presently owned and operated by the Grand Heritage Hotel Group, the Stanley remains the grandest property on either side of the Park. Over the years, it has hosted such prominent guests as J. C. Penney, John Phillip Sousa, Harvey Firestone, Dr. William Mayo, *Titanic* survivor "Unsinkable Molly" Brown, Theodore Roosevelt, the Emperor and Empress of Japan, and many Hollywood personalities. Author Stephen King wrote his famous novel, *The Shining*, after staying at the Stanley, coincidentally setting his spooky story at a grand old hotel in the mountains.

The Stanley Hotel is designated a National Historic Landmark, its elegant Georgian structure standing dramatically against the backdrop of Lumpy Ridge and overlooking a stunning vista of the Estes Valley and the peaks of Rocky Mountain National Park.

Estes Park Tourism Boom

By the turn of the 20th century, the number of ranches, lodges, private cabins, and summer resorts around Estes Park exploded: The Wind River Lodge in 1902, the Horseshoe Inn in 1908, Moraine Lodge and Sprague's Lodge in 1910, the Brinwood and Fern Lodge in 1911, Fall River Lodge in 1915, and Bear Lake Lodge in 1916.

By the time Rocky Mountain was designated a national park, the tourism boom had grown Estes Park into a bustling gateway community offering lodging, food, entertainment, guide services, and supplies.

Photo by W. T. Lee, August 1916, courtesy of U.S. Geological Survey.

One of the early lodges, Horseshoe Inn was built by Willard Ashton in 1908 in Horseshoe Park along Fall River, well within today's Park boundaries. Guests enjoyed views of Mount Chapin, Mount Chiquita, and Ypsilon Mountain. The inn and outbuildings were removed in 1931.

Photo by W. T. Lee, August 1916, courtesy of U.S. Geological Survey.

Most of these accommodations occupied the flat, open terrain of Horseshoe Park, Moraine Park, and the base of Longs Peak—within the boundaries of what would become Rocky Mountain National Park. Through the decades of the 20th century, changing park policy led to removal of structures within the national park, and today little or no evidence remains of these historic hotels.

A Very Grand Lake

On the west side of the Divide, the growth of tourism was much slower. A brief mining boom along the Colorado River in 1880 drew gold seekers by the thousands to the area. The town of Grand Lake mushroomed, becoming the seat of Grand County. But the boom quickly busted, and Grand Lake's importance faded. A high-profile ambush and shootout in the streets of Grand Lake on July 4, 1883, contributed to its slide from grace. The violence was later revealed as a political assassination of two county commissioners and a court clerk by a rival commissioner, a sheriff, and a deputy. The county seat was moved to Hot Sulphur Springs, and the focus in the Grand Lake area shifted to fishing, hiking, and summer tourism.

Camp Wheeler flies the Stars and Stripes —and airs bed linens next to a tent cabin— on a summer day in 1916.
Photo by W. T. Lee, August 1916, courtesy of U.S. Geological Society.

Set against a backdrop of the Continental Divide and the west side of the Front Range, Grand Lake was a worthy scenic destination. The largest natural lake in Colorado, it offered fishing and boating, as well as hiking and wilderness exploration in the surrounding mountains. But getting there in the early 20th century was no easy task. From Denver, it was a long, circuitous route: west up Clear Creek Canyon, a tortuous climb up and over Berthoud Pass, down into Middle Park and northwest along the Fraser River, then east up the Colorado River.

But those who made the trip were enchanted. To serve the growing trade, the Kauffman House opened on the shores of Grand Lake in 1892. The Fairview House, Grand Lake House, Garrison House, and other smaller guesthouses also offered summertime accommodations. Grand Lake Lodge was built in 1921 to cater to the auto tour trade, but only after Fall River Road was opened, connecting both sides of the Park.

At his ranch along the North Fork of the Colorado River, near Milner Pass, Robert Wheeler opened one of the first dude ranches in the area, Camp Wheeler. Nicknamed "Squeaky Bob" for his high-pitched voice, Wheeler was known for his hospitality as well as the rustic nature of his "Hotel de Hardscrabble," which catered mainly to hunters and anglers. A sign on each of the tent cabins read "Blow your nose and clean your shoes." Squeaky Bob reputedly didn't bother with the usual refinements at his guest ranch, such as changing the sheets. He simply freshened the look and smell of the bedding occasionally by sprinkling it liberally with talcum powder. At the end of the summer season, he drove a wagon mounded high with dirty linens to the laundry in Grand Lake.

Robert "Squeaky Bob" Wheeler and his dog Jack greeted visitors to Camp Wheeler, an early dude ranch on the North Fork of the Colorado River on the west side of the Park.
Photo courtesy of Grand Lake Historical Society.

A business card for Camp Wheeler advertises "Good fishing and hunting in season."
Photo courtesy of Grand Lake Historical Society.

A Need to Preserve the Land

In just a few decades, the bourgeoning tourism business left the slopes and valleys on both sides of the Divide marked with hotels, lodges, and roads. Enos Mills and other residents became concerned that the wild character of the landscape was in danger of disappearing beneath a wave of development. This was not only their home but the source of their livelihood. A preserve or refuge of some kind, they decided, was needed to protect the mountain wilderness. It was time for those who loved the mountains to act.

The Kauffman House

Hauling building materials to Grand Lake all the way from Denver by horse-drawn wagon cost a fortune and took three to five days (depending on weather and stops along the way), so enterprising hotelier Ezra Kauffman built his elegant hotel on the shores of Grand Lake from the abundant lodgepole pines growing all around. Split in half lengthwise, then stacked on edge, rounded side out and secured, the logs were chinked on the exterior and plastered on the interior with local clay, then covered with fabric and wallpaper. The hotel's water came directly from Grand Lake, pumped into a cistern and stored.

The Kauffmans opened their hotel in 1892 and hosted guests every summer until 1946. Many visitors returned year after year to stay in their favorite of the four guest rooms, eating their meals family style in the small dining room. In later decades, the hotel fell into disrepair. It was purchased and restored by the Grand Lake Historical Society in 1973. Today, though the creaking floors slope and the walls aren't quite plumb, this charming example of an early log hotel that served visitors to Rocky lives on as a museum on the Grand Lake waterfront.

After Ezra Kauffman died in 1920, his widow, Belle, and their daughters, Ruth, Rosemary, and Margaret, continued to operate the hotel until 1946.
Photo courtesy of Grand Lake Historical Society.

In the early years, guests arrived at the Kauffman House by stagecoach. The trip from Denver took up to five days, depending on weather and road conditions.
Photo courtesy of Grand Lake Historical Society.

Wildflowers thrive in the spray of an alpine waterfall.
Photo by John Fielder.

5

A Fountain of Life:
The Making of a National Park

I T WAS A GLOOMY DAY *for a celebration. Summer was not yet gone, but the air was chilly and the overcast sky threatened rain. A slight drizzle began, then the skies opened up and let loose a downpour. But for the dedicated people who had worked five long years to make this moment a reality, September 4, 1915, was the sunniest day of the year.*

The dignitaries, conservationists, businessmen, tourists, and citizens gathered in Horseshoe Park knew that, despite the weather, this ceremony was very significant—for the local community, for the state of Colorado, and for the country as a whole. Eventually, the clouds broke and the sun shone down on the dedication ceremony welcoming Rocky Mountain National Park as America's tenth national park.

By the turn of the 20th century, development pockmarked the mountains, valleys, and forests around Estes Park and, to a lesser degree, Grand Lake. Concerned that uncontrolled development was ruining the wild character of the mountain landscape, in 1906 local businessmen including F. O. Stanley and Cornelius Bond, the developer of the town of Estes Park, formed the Estes Park Protective and Improvement Association. At that time, the area's publicly owned land was part of the Medicine Bow Forest Reserve, under jurisdiction of the U.S. Forest Service. The reserve's supervisor, H. N. Wheeler, stood before a meeting of the association and planted an

idea. Game animals were the area's greatest tourism asset, he said. Create a game preserve and you'll attract hunters and nature lovers both.

The association voted to support a proposal to create Estes National Park and Game Preserve. The move put into play the significant energy of innkeeper Enos Mills, a naturalist and lecturer of growing

A large crowd braved a blustery day on September 4, 1915, to witness the dedication ceremony for Rocky Mountain National Park.

Photo by Harry Mellon Rhoads, courtesy of Denver Public Library.

An avid mountain climber, author, poet, and musician, Denver attorney James Grafton Rogers (1883–1971) was instrumental in drafting the legislation that ultimately won Rocky's designation as a national park.
NPS photo courtesy of Rocky Mountain National Park Archives.

Known as "the National Park Lady," Mary Belle King Sherman (1862–1935) served as the chair of the Conservation Committee for the General Federation of Women's Clubs from 1914 to 1920. During this time, she helped guide the formation of no fewer than six national parks.
NPS photo courtesy of Rocky Mountain National Park Archives.

renown. Mills took the bit between his teeth and began a campaign to protect the area as a park where visitors could discover and enjoy untrammeled nature. But Mills rejected the concept of a game preserve administered by the Forest Service, whose motto, "Land of Many Uses," encouraged grazing, logging, mining, and other resource development. "Though a Forest Reserve, like a farm, has beauty . . . it is plainly and severely a business proposition as is the growing of wheat and potatoes or the raising of hogs," he wrote. A national park like Yellowstone or Yosemite, which preserved the area for its aesthetic values, was the only thing that would do.

For the Benefit and Enjoyment of the People

Establishing Rocky Mountain National Park became Mills' personal crusade. He wrote more than 2,000 letters, gave 42 lectures, published more than 60 articles for newspapers and magazines, and made more than 400 of his photographs available in support of the effort. Using his platform as a lecturer and writer, he promoted the idea nationwide. He persuaded J. Horace McFarland of the influential American Civic Association to support the idea. Together with Denver attorney James Grafton Rogers and others, he formed the Colorado Mountain Club (CMC) in 1912 as a citizen support group similar to John Muir's Sierra Club.

The campaign to create the Park was not a one-man crusade. Many others worked diligently to make the national park a reality. Rogers and his law partner wrote the legislation, drafting and re-drafting bills for Colorado's delegation to present to Congress. Estes Park locals campaigned for the effort, including Mary Belle King Sherman of the General Federation of Women's Clubs, who became known as "the National Park Lady" for her work to establish six national parks and create the National Park Service. Realizing that a national park would draw tourists from throughout the country, the Denver Chamber of Commerce got on board, as did business and civic groups in Boulder and in Larimer and Grand counties, in which the park would be located. The *Denver Post* supported the effort through editorials and news coverage.

While creation of a national park might seem like something everyone would support, there was strong opposition, particularly from ranching, mining, and timber interests. They wanted continued access to the area's natural resources, which a national forest would allow but a national park would not.

Also complicating the crusade was Mills himself. The flipside of the passionate preservationist was a man with a volatile personality. He attacked opponents and allies alike, often alienating those who were on his side by complaining they were too lackadaisical in their efforts or implying secret complicity with the Forest Service to defeat the park.

Mills' original proposal envisioned a 1,000-square-mile park stretching along the Colorado Front Range from Wyoming to Pikes Peak. It included districts like Central City that had been heavily mined for decades, as well as existing towns, ranches, farms, and homes. The idea of locking up such a vast area from development was a major stumbling block to the park's approval. When Congressman Edward Taylor of Fort Collins presented a bill to create Estes National Park and Game Reserve in 1910, it went nowhere. In 1912, Robert Marshall, chief geographer of the U.S.

Geological Survey, visited the area and recommended, "for the benefit and enjoyment of the people a National Park in the Rocky Mountains of Colorado in the vicinity of Longs Peak to be known as Rocky Mountain National Park." In his recommendation, he pared down Mills' vision of a super-sized park to 700 square miles.

In 1913, the first bill to create Rocky Mountain National Park was presented to Congress. It never made it out of committee. Rogers re-drafted the legislation, but the second bill got no further. In 1914, with additional compromise on acreage, Congressman Taylor and Senator Charles Thomas shepherded a third bill through the House and Senate. Three Colorado governors—former governor John Shafroth, then-governor Elias Ammons, and governor-elect George Carlson—all testified in favor of the bill, as did Enos Mills and other prominent Coloradans.

Finally, on January 18, 1915, the third bill passed Congress. It had taken five years of lobbying, debate,

Among the notables present for Rocky's dedication were, from left to right between the trees, Stephen Mather (soon to be director of the National Park Service), newspaper editor and national park publicity chief Robert Sterling Yard, then-acting park superintendent C. R. Trowbridge, first national park photographer Herford Cowling, and Mather's right-hand-man, Horace M. Albright.

NPS photo courtesy of Rocky Mountain National Park Archives.

conflict, and compromise, and, at 358.5 square miles, the new park encompassed only a third of the land Enos Mills originally envisioned. But it had happened. On January 26, 1915, President Woodrow Wilson signed the bill into law. Rocky Mountain National Park was born.

Dedication Day

With the park a reality, its supporters were ready to celebrate. In spite of the drizzly weather, some 300 people gathered in Horseshoe Park beneath a banner that read, "Rocky Mountain Nat'l Park—Dedication, Sept. 4, 1915." Enos Mills was master of ceremonies. "I have lived to see the great realization of a dream come true," he told the crowd. "In years to come when I am asleep forever beneath the pines, thousands of families will find rest and hope in this park."

Others who had worked hard to establish the Park were there—James Grafton Rogers, F. O. Stanley, national parks activist Mary Sherman—and dignitaries including Colorado governor George Carlson and Stephen Mather, associate secretary of the Department of the Interior. Mather soon became the first director of the National Park Service upon its creation in 1916.

It wasn't a perfect mountain day, but even the eventual downpour couldn't put a damper on the

Enos Mills' workshop at Longs Peak Inn afforded splendid views of its namesake peak, just four miles distant.
Photo by Robert. B. Marshall, 1912, courtesy of U.S. Geological Survey.

Photographer William Lee confers with Enos Mills at Longs Peak Inn. Lee and Mills shared a passion for both mountains and photography.
Photo by W. T. Lee, July 27, 1916, courtesy of U.S. Geological Survey.

significance of the moment as an outstanding portion of the Colorado Rocky Mountains was preserved for the people of the United States.

Rocky's Tireless Campaigner

Creation of Rocky Mountain National Park came about through the dedication and determined work of many people and organizations, but its most tireless advocate, and the man who was the public face of the effort, was naturalist and innkeeper Enos Mills.

In classic American style, the man who the *Denver Post* dubbed "the Father of Rocky Mountain National Park" had humble beginnings. Enos Abijah Mills was born on a Quaker farm near Pleasanton, Kansas, on April 22, 1870. He was a sickly boy, and at age fourteen, his parents sent him to live with relatives in Estes Park, hoping he would benefit from a healthier climate. Mills' cousins, Reverend and Mrs. Elkanah Lamb and their son, Carlyle, operated a ranch, hotel, and guide service at the foot of Longs Peak. Young Enos took quickly to the robust mountain life. In 1885, at just fifteen, he began work on a homestead cabin in the Tahosa Valley

at the foot of Twin Sisters Peak. That same year, he climbed Longs Peak for the first time. It was the beginning of a lifelong love affair with the mountain—which he climbed more than 250 times—and the wild and wonderful world of nature surrounding it.

A chance meeting during an 1889 visit to San Francisco set Mills on the course that would become his legacy. Walking on the beach, he became intrigued by a clump of kelp and stopped a passerby to ask about it. The man was famous naturalist and writer John Muir, founder of the Sierra Club and a key player in the founding of Yosemite, Sequoia, Mount Rainier, and Petrified Forest National Parks. In spite of the age difference—Mills was just nineteen and Muir in his fifties—the two men became friends. Muir triggered in Mills a passion for preserving the natural world, which was already under threat in the West by rampant settlement and development. Muir encouraged Mills to write about his nature experiences to inspire others to support wilderness conservation.

Back in Estes Park, Mills purchased the Lamb Ranch, changing the name of their lodge, the

Despite the volatile mountain weather, guests for Rocky's dedication arrived by automobile, motorcycle, horseback, and on foot.
Photo courtesy of Grand Lake Historical Society.

Longs Peak House, to the Longs Peak Inn. Wearing the hats of innkeeper and nature guide, he led guests on walks and peak climbs, extolling the beauties of nature and trying to inspire a passion for preserving it. He greeted visitors on beautiful summer mornings with a cheery, "Glad you're living?" But innkeeping was a summertime endeavor, and Mills took a winter job as an official Snow Observer for the Department of Agriculture, snowshoeing into the Rockies to measure snow depth, an indicator used to predict spring runoff. He also became a traveling lecturer on forestry.

Enos' lectures that began as evening campfire talks at the Longs Peak Inn evolved into public programs in support of establishing Rocky Mountain National Park. Following Muir's advice, Mills began writing articles and books about the natural world. Busy with writing and speaking engagements, Enos soon had little time for leading nature walks and hikes. He opened a Trail School to train nature guides to cater to his guests. His techniques, stressing discovery rather than identification, became the basis for the fledgling field of nature interpretation, and he is often considered the founder of the naturalist profession. "A wilderness becomes a wonderland with a nature guide," he wrote.

The idea of creating a national park to preserve the mountains of the Front Range became Mills' consuming mission. "A national park," he wrote, "is a fountain of life . . . . It holds within its magic realm benefits that are health-giving . . . . Without parks and outdoor life all that is best in civilization will be smothered."

He was single-minded in his commitment, writing thousands of letters, lecturing tirelessly, and lobbying and testifying before Congress. His mercurial personality

In his work as a nature guide, Enos Mills enjoyed encouraging children's appreciation for the mountains he loved.
Photo courtesy of Library of Congress (LC-USZ62-105647).

often led him into conflict. In his eyes, the Forest Service became the enemy when its director opposed turning the area into a park whose timber, mineral, and other resources would be off-limits to harvest and development. Mills even criticized allies who did not campaign as diligently as he did or who seemed willing to make concessions with the Forest Service.

In 1916, a year after Rocky Mountain National Park became a reality, twenty-five-year-old Esther Burnell came to Estes Park for a vacation and stayed to homestead. She caught the eye of Enos Mills after she snowshoed across the Continental Divide to visit friends in Grand Lake. Esther worked as a naturalist at the Longs Peak Inn and also for a while as Enos' secretary.

Enos and Esther married in 1918 and had one daughter, Enda. Sadly, the little girl would only know her father for a few years. Mills died in 1922 at the age of fifty-two from blood poisoning that developed from an infected tooth. Esther spread his ashes in the mountains he loved and had fought so passionately to preserve. She operated Longs Peak Inn until 1946 and died in 1964. Enos' original log cabin, built in 1885, is listed on the National Register of Historic Places. It is still owned by the Mills family, who operate it as a museum.

One might wonder what the land between Estes Park and Grand Lake would be like today without Enos Mills' commitment to the national park crusade. His accomplishments as innkeeper, author, lecturer, photographer, and pioneer naturalist might have been enough for many men. But Mills had an all-consuming love of the mountains and the natural world. He may have been eccentric and combative, but his impassioned efforts helped preserve a stunning part of the Rocky Mountains for the enjoyment of all Americans.

Enos Mills' life in the mountains provided ample opportunities for studying, photographing, and writing about nature.
Photo by W. T. Lee, 1916, courtesy of U.S. Geological Survey.

No Fans of the National Park

Self-reliant, resourceful homesteaders, Kitty (left) and Annie (right) Harbison worked their dairy farm on Rocky's west side for nearly four decades.
Photo courtesy of Grand Lake Historical Society.

Winters at the Harbison Ranch brought cold temperatures and deep snows typical of the mountain valleys on the west side of the Continental Divide.
Photo courtesy of Grand Lake Historical Society.

The Harbisons used this "beaverslide" haystacker to pile hay as high as 30 feet. One team of horses brought hay to the slide in a buckrake, where it was placed in a basket attached to cables on pulleys. Another team pulled the cables to raise the basket, gradually building the haystack. The sheer size of the haystack protects most of the hay from weather and rot for up to two years.
Photo courtesy of Grand Lake Historical Society.

Not everyone celebrated the dedication of the new national park. Two self-reliant sisters who homesteaded in the Kawuneeche Valley looked askance at having the federal government as a neighbor and resisted selling their ranch to the Park Service for many years.

Annie and Kitty Harbison arrived in Grand Lake in 1895 with their family. They and their stepbrother filed for homesteads on neighboring tracts of land along the Colorado River about a mile northwest of Grand Lake. Each built a cabin on either side of their mutual property line, just 100 feet apart. In between they built The Big Cabin, where the family, including their mother and brother Rob, lived. They used Annie's cabin as kitchen space, but never connected the close-set buildings. The sisters

cleared trees, built fences, wrangled horses, and cut hay in the big meadow along the Colorado. They operated a herd of thirty to forty dairy cows, delivering milk and butter to customers in Grand Lake. They began taking in paying guests, eventually building a few tourist cabins and offering elaborate Sunday dinners for $1.

After Rocky was established, the Park Service tried to purchase some of the Harbisons' property to build an entrance road into the new Park. The sisters demanded $30,000 for their ranch, an enormous sum for the time. Not until 1938 did they agree to sell a carefully surveyed corner of the ranch as a right-of-way for the western end of Trail Ridge Road. Kitty, who was nearly seventy, rode out on horseback to locate the exact corners of the parcel, then went out again on skis in the middle of winter, digging through deep snow to reconfirm the boundaries. Later that year, the two sisters both died of pneumonia within a few days of each other.

The sisters' adopted daughter continued to operate the ranch until the mid-1950s, when she sold the remaining property to the Park. Kitty and Annie's cabins and other ranch buildings became the west-side maintenance yard. Despite calls for their preservation, the old ranch buildings languished and fell into disrepair, and in 1973 were razed. Evidence of the Harbison years in the Kawuneeche Valley survives only in the name of the Harbison Meadows Picnic Area, which overlooks their former cow pasture.

Annie Harbison's homestead patent (left), dated December 30, 1902, grants ownership to 160 acres, while Kitty's claim (below) was for an adjoining 162.66 acres.
Photo courtesy of Grand Lake Historical Society.

After the Harbison land was sold to the Park, the cabins fell into disrepair and were razed in 1973.
Photo courtesy of Grand Lake Historical Society.

*Wildflowers stream through
a lush mountain meadow.*
Photo by John Fielder

6

A Park for the Automobile Age

T HE DRIVER OF THE MODEL T *steamed as furiously as his overheating automobile. Attempting to navigate the new Fall River Road up to the crest of Rocky Mountain National Park, he was stymied by a switchback tighter than grandma's hairpin. The only way to make the curve was to trundle forward a few feet, crank the wheel and reverse, trundle forward again, and reverse, until the car could navigate the turn.*

To make things worse, there was no barrier to keep his car from plunging down the steep embankment if he trundled backward too far. What the driver didn't know was that further challenges awaited him. He would need to honk at every curve to warn oncoming vehicles. Some of the inclines ahead were so steep that gasoline, relying on gravity feed, would drain away from the engine, causing it to conk out. To make it all the way to Fall River Pass, he would have to turn his car around in places and back it up the road.

When Rocky Mountain National Park opened in 1915, it was different from parks like Yellowstone, Yosemite, or Glacier, where most tourists arrived by rail. No railroad served the new park. Visitors to Rocky would come by car.

At the same time that Rocky was opening its gates, America was beginning its love affair with the automobile. It was a match made in heaven. Car-happy tourists were more than ready to motor along to the new national park that lay just sixty-five miles from Denver. In 1916, the new park hosted 51,000 visitors. But there was a snag. The existing roads dead-ended just two miles into the Park. A vast expanse of forest, tundra, peaks, and vistas beckoned, with no easy way to see them.

Fall River Road

Even before establishment of the Park, business and civic interests in Estes Park and Grand Lake realized

Completed in September 1920, Fall River Road was a narrow dirt and gravel track, but it linked the Park from east to west, traversing the Continental Divide.
Photo courtesy of Grand Lake Historical Society.

that for tourism to grow there had to be an auto route across the Continental Divide. In 1913, the state of Colorado, together with Larimer and Grand counties, began construction of a road that would travel from Estes Park up along Fall River, over Fall River Pass, then down into the Kawuneeche Valley to link up with the road to Grand Lake.

Construction would be a long process. The first year, convict labor was brought in from the state prison at Cañon City. The men lived in rough cabins in Endovalley at what is still the beginning point of Fall River Road. But after two years of work, they had completed only two miles of road. Private contractors replaced the convicts, but a shortage of labor due

to World War I continued to slow progress. Finally, with more money and the acquisition of heavy equipment, the thirty-seven-mile road was completed and opened in September of 1920.

With access between both sides of the Park, visitation surged. By 1921, Rocky was the most popular national park in the country, hosting nearly 280,000 visitors—more than Yellowstone, Yosemite, Glacier, and Crater Lake national parks combined.

But all wasn't rosy. Fall River Road was narrow, only eight to ten feet wide in some places, and unpaved. Its gravel surface became a muddy morass during spring melt or after summer rain showers. There were hairpin turns and steep, engine-killing inclines. Fall River

Drivers braving Fall River Road had to contend with mud, rockfalls, abrupt edges, and—as shown in this July 4, 1926, image—narrow cuts through deep snow.
Photo courtesy of Grand Lake Historical Society.

A caravan of cars lines the road, with Mount Ypsilon in the background. With accessibility by automobile, Rocky's scenery proved irresistible.
NPS photo courtesy of Rocky Mountain National Park Archives.

"was not a road for timid drivers," wrote one author. Rangers were stationed along the road to drive the cars of tourists who became intimidated by the tight turns and steep drop-offs. Deep snow, avalanches, and snowslides made clearing the road in spring a monumental task. Lacking appropriate equipment, crews shoveled by hand through drifts up to nineteen feet high. Dynamite was used to loosen deep, hard-packed snow.

Within four years of opening, Fall River Road was deemed obsolete. "Numerous complaints on road conditions have been received in this office," wrote the Park's chief ranger, R. A. Kennedy. "Unless funds are soon provided, conditions will become so deplorable that pleasurable traffic will be impossible."

In 1924, Congress came to the rescue, prodded along by National Park Service Director Stephen Mather. Mather envisioned a highway route, the Park-to-Park Highway, that would take visitors on a grand road tour of twelve western national parks. He convinced Congress to appropriate $7.5 million to build roads in national parks. Rocky Mountain National Park could finally construct a road that would truly meet visitor needs while providing an unequalled showcase for the Park's outstanding scenery.

Highway to Heaven: Trail Ridge Road

Local businesses wanted it, tourists wanted it, the Park Service wanted it—a safe, functional road between Estes Park and Grand Lake. But while the

Cars thread across Rocky's tundra on Trail Ridge Road.
NPS photo by Ann Schonlau, courtesy of Rocky Mountain National Park Archives.

federal government had the money to build the road, it didn't have legal jurisdiction. Finally in 1929, five years after the funds were allocated to build a new road, the state of Colorado and Grand and Larimer counties ceded control over roads within the Park to the National Park Service. The agency had $450,000 to build a route that would bypass Fall River Road altogether. The new road would wind gradually up and along Trail Ridge, following portions of the ancient Ute Trail used by native people for thousands of years to travel between Middle Park and Colorado's Eastern Plains.

In October 1929, construction began on Trail Ridge Road. One crew, under contractor W. A. Colt of Las Animas, Colorado, began working from the east side. In spite of high winds, snow, thin air, and other difficulties encountered at 11,000 feet, including permafrost tundra that resisted drilling and grading, they built more than half of their seventeen miles of road by September of the next year. Colt's progress allowed opening of the east side of Trail Ridge Road, as far as Fall River Pass, by July 1932.

Meanwhile, contractor L. T. Lawler of Butte, Montana, began working from the west on eleven miles of road from the Kawuneeche Valley to Fall River

Summer comes late at an elevation of 11,796 feet, and the Alpine Visitor Center often remains shrouded in snow long after Trail Ridge Road has been cleared by plows.
NPS photo courtesy of Rocky Mountain National Park Archives.

In its early days, the western end of Trail Ridge Road was a rough, one-lane track into the mountains.
Photo courtesy of Grand Lake Historical Society.

A truck-mounted derrick moves heavy boulders during construction of Trail Ridge Road in 1929.
NPS photo courtesy of Rocky Mountain National Park Archives.

Pass, where it would link with Colt's road. Unusually snowy winters slowed their progress but, with a few final touches still pending, Trail Ridge Road opened to through traffic in the summer of 1935. The project was completed on time, within budget, and without loss of life.

Trail Ridge Road has survived for eighty years because of meticulous planning. Meandering with the contours of the landscape so as to be as unobtrusive as possible, it has no grades greater than seven percent. Anticipating that future vehicles would likely be larger than the Model T's of their day, planners made the road twenty-four feet wide, shoulder-to-shoulder, and wider on curves. They gave blind curves a radius of 200 feet, open curves, 100 feet.

In what seems very forward-thinking for their time, the road's builders worked hard to preserve the scenic beauty and natural values of the landscape. After all, destroying the scenery through which they were building a road to bring people to enjoy made no sense. The contractors built latticeworks of

wooden poles to protect vulnerable rock pillars and the age-old lichens growing on them. They constructed rock walls to minimize scarring from blast debris and carefully picked up rocks strewn by blasting. They built windrows of logs or rocks at the base of slopes to catch displaced material, set overturned boulders back in place lichen side up, and carefully salvaged tundra sod and placed it along road banks. Instead of removing rock outcrops, the builders kept them as "window frames" for the view. Crews built retaining walls out of local rock to match the landscape.

With the opening of Trail Ridge Road, American tourists again flocked to the Park, eager to drive across the breathtaking road nicknamed "the Highway to Heaven." In 1936, in spite of the Great Depression, visitation to Rocky hit 550,496. It continued to climb until the beginning of World War II.

Today, three-quarters of all Park visitors travel Trail Ridge Road, delighting at the views and the alpine landscape they would probably never see otherwise. Trail Ridge remains the highest continuous

Glass-domed tour buses await passengers at Grand Lake Lodge during the summer of 1956.
NPS photo courtesy of Rocky Mountain National Park Archives.

paved highway in the country, reaching its top elevation—12,183 feet—between the Lava Cliffs and the Alpine Visitor Center. Roads to the summits of Pikes Peak and Mount Evans reach a higher altitude, but also dead-end there. Eleven of Trail Ridge Road's nearly thirty miles lie above timberline. The drive from Estes Park to the Alpine Visitor Center rises nearly 4,000 feet in elevation, from montane pine forests to alpine tundra. Some visitors describe it as akin to going from Colorado to Alaska all in one day!

The First Big Conflict: The Transportation Contract

Not all tourists wanted to drive their own vehicles to visit Rocky, and many tour companies stood ready and eager to carry paying customers into the new park. But in 1919, the Park's superintendent, L. C. Way, granted an exclusive, no-bid contract to commercially transport tourists within the Park to Rocky Mountain Parks Transportation Company, owned by Roe Emery. Even local hotels could not drive their guests into the park. An immediate furor erupted, the most vehement opponent being Enos Mills. Having fought for years to create this very park, hotel owner

Mills was outraged. The exclusive deal went against both competitive business principles and his notions that a national park should be easily accessible to everyone. In violation of the new ruling, Mills sent one of the Longs Peak Inn's vehicles, with several passengers, into the Park. When they were stopped on Fall River Road and booted out—by Superintendent Way personally—Mills sued, challenging the right of the two-year-old National Park Service to limit travel on roads that were still legally owned by the state and counties. Sadly, the controversy led to bad blood between Enos Mills and the administration of the Park he was considered father of. The issues he raised led directly into road jurisdiction issues that were not settled until after Mills' death in 1922, with the ceding of all Park roads to the federal government.

The Circle Tour

With his transportation concession contract, Roe Emery and his Rocky Mountain Parks Transportation Company began an ambitious plan that went far beyond driving hotel guests in and out of the Park. He established The Circle Tour, a multi-night auto tour that would prove enormously popular.

Inside and out, the design of Grand Lake Lodge embraces themes common to other lodges associated with national parks: exposed timbers, native stone, and rustic touches, such as fixtures made of elk antlers.
NPS photo courtesy of Rocky Mountain National Park Archives.

The Circle Tour began in Denver, where it picked up passengers in touring buses and brought them to the Lewiston Chalet (later the Marys Lake Lodge) on the east side of the Park. The next morning they headed up the scenic but often nail-biting Fall River Road—some of the passengers hiding their eyes and clinging to the seats at the hairier turns—and across the tundra to the head of the Kawuneeche Valley. Down along the Colorado River they went, to Grand Lake, for their second night. Here Emery had partnered with A. D. Lewis, owner of the Lewiston Chalet, to construct the Grand Lake Lodge specifically to house Circle Tour guests in grand style. The lodge, still in operation, is a classic, national park-style hotel with guest cabins, its main building a single open space with massive beams. After a comfortable night and a morning spent taking in the view of Grand Lake and surrounding mountains from the hotel's porch, guests once again loaded into touring buses to traverse the harrowing road up and over Berthoud Pass. In Idaho Springs, they spent a third night at the Hot Springs Hotel before completing the tour back to Denver.

Over time, Emery purchased all three hotels in The Circle Tour. He expanded his operation to pick up guests at train stations in Greeley and Lyons. In 1953, he sold his hotels and the transportation company to Ted and Isaac James of Nebraska. Grand Lake Lodge was built on Park land, but in 1963 the James brothers successfully negotiated with the Park Service to change the Park boundary to remove the lodge and its seventy-two acres from the Park. Thus the Grand Lake Lodge escaped the fate of other hotels within the Park, which were acquired by the Park Service and razed. It remains the lone example of a national park-style lodge around Rocky Mountain National Park and is listed on the National Register of Historic Places.

Dawn of the MOtor hoTEL

The automobile changed not only how Americans arrived at Rocky, but where and for how long they stayed. Cars introduced the age of the motor hotel, or motel. Instead of checking in to a grand, multi-room hotel for a lengthy stay, many travelers now wanted a no-frills place to spend one or two nights, with their car parked conveniently by the door. The first motel in America—the Cottage Court—opened in Grand Lake just outside the west boundary of the national park.

Johnnie Holzwarth and Hal Simonds cut hay with a horse-drawn swather.

Photo courtesy of Grand Lake Historical Society.

In 1915, Grand Lake hotelier Preston Smith, sensing a change in how tourists traveled, established the Cottage Court as a simple, park-and-stay lodging. The Court's four one-room cabins were connected by carports. Guests needed to travel only a few steps from the door of their room to their car. Each rustic, bark-sided cabin featured a wood stove for heat, a bed, chair, small table, and curtained closet area. The bathroom and laundry were in a separate building. In 1947, a room rented for $1.50 per night.

Smith's grandson, Clyde Eslick, and his wife, Grace, operated the property until the late 1960s. Over the years, the motel fell into disrepair. The Grand Lake Historical Society acquired the property and relocated the buildings to prevent their demolition. A major effort to restore the Cottage Court with early motel furnishings is underway, in association with a proposed Grand Lake History Park.

Holzwarth Ranch

As auto tourism began taking off in the new national park, the Holzwarth family saw an opportunity to turn their hardscrabble life as Kawuneeche Valley ranchers into a more profitable venture as innkeepers and fishing guides. They opened their homestead along the west side of the Colorado River to visitors in the 1920s as the Holzwarth Trout Lodge. By 1923, as the Fall River Road brought more and more tourists over the Divide and past their doors, they built a roomy log lodge on the east side of the river and expanded into the dude ranch business. Their Never Summer Ranch gave visitors a taste of the cowboy life, taking them on horse trips through the mountains of Rocky Mountain National Park. After more than forty years of hosting guests, Johnnie Holzwarth ensured his family's legacy when he sold the ranch to The Nature Conservancy in 1974. Acquired by the Park Service, the original log buildings of the Holzwarth Trout Lodge remain as the Holzwarth Historic Site, where park volunteers tell stories of early 20th-century tourism at the ranch. Visitors can tour the "Mama Cabin" and other buildings, still outfitted with artifacts owned by the Holzwarths.

The Never Summer Ranch lodge and other modern buildings, once located in the meadow by the river, were removed to restore the site to a more natural state.

Johnnie Holzwarth, right, helped preserve the ranch in perpetuity by selling it to The Nature Conservancy in 1974.

NPS photo courtesy of Rocky Mountain National Park Archives.

Sophie "Mama" Holzwarth prepared hearty meals in the kitchen of the "Mama Cabin," serving local trout, venison, and grouse, along with the ranch's own chickens, eggs, and milk.

Photo courtesy of Grand Lake Historical Society.

Horses cavort at the Holzwarth's Never Summer Ranch in the Kawuneeche Valley.
Photo courtesy of Grand Lake Historical Society.

A Holzwarth ranch hand ropes a calf. Guests staying at Never Summer Ranch reveled in the old western ways.
Photo courtesy of Grand Lake Historical Society.

A highlight of any stay at Never Summer Ranch was a trail ride into the mountains.
Photo courtesy of Grand Lake Historical Society.

The Park Service maintains the original Holzwarth homestead cabin, preserving it for generations of visitors to come.
Photo courtesy of Grand Lake Historical Society.

Nestled in the Kawuneeche Valley below the cut of the Grand Ditch, the Holzwarth ranch gave early visitors a respite from the summer heat.
NPS photo courtesy of Rocky Mountain National Park Archives.

Summer blooms climb a ridge in Rocky.
Photo by Erik Stensland.

7

Ups and Downs:
The Depression and World War II

"THEY SAY THE NEW DEAL *brings luck. It brought it to me. A few months ago I was broke. At this writing I am sitting on top of the world. Almost literally so, because National Park No. 1 CCC Camp near Estes Park is 9,000 feet up. Instead of holding down a park bench or pounding the pavements looking for work, today I have work, plenty of good food, and a view of the sort that people pay money to see. We are going to have a Hamburg steak tonight. And I am on the payroll."*

— a Civilian Conservation Corps enrollee working in Rocky Mountain
National Park, quoted in *Liberty* magazine, May 5, 1934.

The Great Depression of the 1930s brought hard times for the country but some benefits for Rocky Mountain National Park. Visitation actually increased, and government efforts to create jobs through the Civilian Conservation Corps brought an army of workers into the Park to build and improve infrastructure, much of it still in use today.

The Green Guard:
The CCC Comes to the Park

In 1933, President Franklin D. Roosevelt pushed a bill through Congress creating the Civilian Conservation Corps, or CCC, to provide jobs for unemployed young men. Dubbed "the Green Guard of the Roosevelt Revolution," the CCC worked in national parks and

Despite the Great Depression, visitors flocked to Rocky during the 1930s, here filling the parking lot at the Fall River Pass Museum.

NPS photo courtesy of Rocky Mountain National Park Archives.

national forests on projects that conserved the country's natural resources.

A spring blizzard greeted the CCC advance guard as they arrived in Little Horseshoe Park in May 1933. Undaunted, they set to work shoveling snow and erecting a tent city to house the 159 men following on their heels. But the men arrived before most of the supplies needed to house, clothe, and feed them. The CCC intended to operate along military lines, but enrollees were average citizens, not trained soldiers. Hungry and shivering in their drafty tents in the snow, they rioted. The Park Service opened the out-of-use Moraine Lodge to give them shelter, and the men endured until the supplies finally arrived. But just as they'd finally settled into their tent encampment, another late-spring blizzard howled through, shredding the tents and blowing pots, pans, and other gear down the valley. Perhaps hardened by their earlier experience, the now well-fed and warmly clothed

men hung on. Within a day, the camp was back in business, and the men embarked on their first conservation mission—cutting down beetle-killed trees from the Park's forests.

Camp Number One, in Little Horseshoe Park, included rows of tents laid out along a single street with an infirmary, mess hall, bathhouse, and latrines. The camp was run by the U.S. Army, and the CCC operated like the military. Enrollees had to be unemployed, unmarried, physically fit, and between the ages of eighteen and twenty-five. They earned $1 a day, plus clothing, food, and housing, with $25 of their monthly pay usually sent home to the family. Foremen and "straw bosses" could be older and married, and earned more.

The men—ranging from cowhands to college students—were there to do hard physical work. The camp cooks fed them well, probably much better than some of them were accustomed to. The CCC

CCC cooks prepared well-rounded meals for the men, many of whom had suffered through lean times.
NPS photo courtesy of Rocky Mountain National Park Archives.

issued each man two pairs of denim pants, one pair of khaki pants, two khaki shirts, a denim hat, two pairs of boots, and six pairs of socks. Each man also received a canteen, tin mess kit, and bedding. Because of the altitude and cold weather, workers in Rocky received six blankets instead of the customary four, and mattresses stuffed with cotton instead of straw.

Battell Loomis, an unemployed magazine writer who joined the CCC in Rocky Mountain National Park, later recalled his CCC days:

Up at six o'clock in the morning. Breakfast—hot and plenty of it—at seven. Camp police from seven thirty to eight. Then off to work for four hours. Lunch at twelve—plenty of it (we get a pound of bread and a pound of meat per man per day, as well as eggs and plenty of vegetables)—followed by four more hours of work. Back in camp by four thirty . . . Each day a few of us get leave to go to town, and week-end leave to visit families is also handled in rotation. No liquor is the hard-and-fast rule.

After the work day, the men played baseball or took it easy. There were also evening classes in English, math, wood and leather working, auto mechanics, and radio.

Eventually, five CCC camps operated on both sides of the Park. Workers built much of the Park's infrastructure that is still in use today. In a 1942 memorandum, Park superintendent David Canfield listed the CCC's accomplishments: construction of two bridges, thirty-three new buildings, 43 miles of trails, seven sewer treatment plants, 465 miles of utility lines, 8 miles of water lines, three amphitheaters, fish ponds, rock walls, reservoirs, and landscaping. The men performed maintenance on 316 miles of roads and 432 miles of trails, fought seven forest fires, and helped in several search-and-rescue operations. In addition, they planted 2,565 trees and shrubs, mitigated for bark beetles over 37,315 acres of forest, and

A CCC construction crew works to install a culvert.
NPS photo courtesy of Rocky Mountain National Park Archives.

CCC camps, like this one in Phantom Valley, were fairly spartan, but the workers were grateful for three square meals a day and the opportunity to learn a trade.
NPS photo courtesy of Rocky Mountain National Park Archives.

placed 1.5 million trout in Park waters. Contrary to popular thought, the CCC did not build Trail Ridge Road, which was constructed by a private contractor.

Up to 75 percent of CCC enrollees working in Rocky were native Coloradans. The CCC program contributed $56 million directly to the Colorado economy through pay to workers in camps statewide.

The attack on Pearl Harbor in December 1941 created a need for American men to fight World War II. The last CCC workers left Rocky in July 1942 and the CCC was disbanded. The skills, physical fitness, and military discipline of CCC workers made them valuable soldiers for America's war effort.

The last task of the CCC men was to dismantle and erase the evidence of their camps. Some of the buildings were moved to the Park's utility area and are still used as employee housing. Nothing remains in Horseshoe Park or any of the other sites to indicate the once-booming camps of workers in Rocky.

The sturdily built products of the CCC's labor, however, remain very much in evidence today. Current Park visitors have likely hiked on or driven past this

Even the Great Depression couldn't keep visitors away. This young woman has dinner on the line —a healthy rainbow trout from the Big Thompson River in Moraine Park.

Photo by Allan Rinehart, 1938, courtesy of NPS Harpers Ferry Center (HPC-000741, Wa. 1039).

work without realizing that many trails, campgrounds, overlooks, and other improvements on both sides of the Park date from this eighty-year-old initiative, which created work for unemployed Americans and improved this and other national parks for everyone.

"Stay"-cation, 1930s Style

Even during the deepest years of the Great Depression, tourists kept coming to Rocky. Visitation more than tripled, from 205,000 in 1933 to 1938, when 660,000 visitors toured the Park. This may reflect an early version of the "stay"-cation trend of the early 2000s, when Americans passed on costly, faraway vacations in favor of inexpensive jaunts close to home. Unlike Yellowstone and Yosemite, whose remote locations meant travelers had to spend at least one night, Rocky was within sixty-five miles of Denver, so visitors could come just for the day. The partial opening of Trail Ridge Road in 1932—from the east as far as Fall River Pass—and the entire road opening in 1935, drew carloads of tourists eager to see the magnificent views and drive "the Highway to Heaven." Those who did spend the night found many affordable "mom-and-pop" hotels in Estes Park and Grand Lake, unlike the grand, national park-style lodges of the other parks.

Eventually, world events caught up with the Park. From a record 685,393 visitors in 1941, Rocky saw an eighty-one percent decrease in visitation by 1943 as the country turned its resources to fighting World War II.

Expanding the Park and Returning It to "Natural"

Soon after the creation of Rocky Mountain National Park in 1915, the Park's boundaries were expanded to include land around Gem Lake, Twin Sisters, and Deer Mountain. In 1930, the Park Service acquired the Never Summer Range along the Park's west side, an area of just over twenty-two square miles that included the headwaters of the Colorado River and the dramatically named Mounts Cumulus, Nimbus, and Cirrus. But hundreds of private inholdings still fragmented the Park.

At the time Rocky was created, many hotels and

Visitors savor the view of Longs Peak from Many Parks Curve, Trail Ridge Road, 1931.
NPS photo courtesy of Rocky Mountain National Park Archives.

Campers prepare breakfast in Aspenglen Campground in the 1930s.
NPS photo courtesy of Rocky Mountain National Park Archives.

Movin' Snow

Snowdrifts such as this one at Rock Cut on Trail Ridge Road are often as tall as the plow.
NPS photo courtesy of Rocky Mountain National Park Archives.

In spite of the Depression, or perhaps seeking diversion from it, visitors descended on the Park by the thousands in the 1930s. The big attraction was the newly opened Trail Ridge Road. But building this Park headliner was only the first part of the battle. Getting it open for business every year was the real work. Clearing Trail Ridge Road of snow and making it passable in the spring was an ever-challenging job. Hand-shoveling, as had been done on Fall River Road, would

The Snogo with its spiral blade throws snow from Trail Ridge Road.
Photo by Fred Clatworthy, 1938, courtesy of History Colorado (Scan # 20010434).

not work. In 1932, the Park set to work with a Snogo, an experimental rotary snow-clearing machine that was essentially a huge snowblower. Innovative for its time, it featured an enclosed cab, four-wheel drive, and roll-up windows. Its six-cylinder, 175-horsepower engine could move the rotary machine at speeds from one-quarter mile per hour when pushing snow, to twenty-five miles per hour when not pushing snow. It reportedly threw snow to the side as far as 100 feet.

The machine worked very well, unless the snow was deeper than forty-five inches. Then the old snow had to be blasted first with dynamite to loosen it so that it would fall into the opening of the machine. The Snogo was retired in 1952 and is listed on the National Register of Historic Places. It is in storage, well protected from the elements.

Today, plowing to open Trail Ridge begins in mid-April and takes an average of forty-two days to complete. A "pioneer" rotary plow clears the center of the road, while a second rotary follows, widening the track. A grader and bulldozer push snow from the uphill side of the road toward the edge, where it melts more quickly. If drifts are more than twenty feet high, a caterpillar climbs up on them and knocks down the snow—which can be a nail-biting job for the operator!

A rotary plow chews into a snowbank on Trail Ridge Road.
NPS photo by John Marino, courtesy of Rocky Mountain National Park Archives.

Engineers met the challenges of building Trail Ridge Road with artful grace as well as technical adroitness.

Photo courtesy of Library of Congress (HAER COLO, 35-ESPK.V,7-16).

The Moraine Park Museum, formerly the recreation hall at Moraine Lodge, opened in 1937 and proved popular with visitors through the war years. The building is now the Moraine Park Visitor Center.

NPS photo courtesy of Rocky Mountain National Park Archives.

businesses that predated the national park were in operation within Park boundaries. When the country fell on hard times during the Great Depression, so did many of these businesses. Though Park visitation increased, most of the visitors came on day trips and did not stay the night. While the downturn hurt the hospitality industry, it created an opportunity for the Park Service to consolidate land and move the Park back to a more natural state.

The first lodging property to sell out to the Park Service was the Horseshoe Inn in Horseshoe Park, in operation since 1909. Its owners sold for $32,500 in 1931. One year later, the Park purchased Moraine Lodge and had CCC workers demolish all the buildings except for the recreation hall. Renovated to a new use, it was opened in 1937 as the Moraine Park Museum. Over the next few years, the Park Service added more than 9,000 acres of inholdings to the Park. Dozens of cabins, lodges, hotels, and other buildings were demolished, the beginning of many removals in a conscious "back-to-nature" effort by Park management. "Our ideals contemplate a national park system of primitive lands free from all present and future commercial utilization," said NPS director Horace Albright. Unsightly development on the periphery and within national parks would make for an unsatisfactory visitor experience. "The establishment of hot dog stands and billboards is frowned upon."

"Most of those who have sold so far are quite happy about the situation," wrote Charles Hewes, owner of the Hewes-Kirkwood Inn, in 1931. He named declining business, high debt, and aging property owners as the reasons for selling. In the decades after World War II, the effort to return Rocky Mountain National Park to a wilder, more natural state continued in earnest.

The War Years

Immediately following the outbreak of World War II, visitation to Rocky began to plummet. In 1943, it dropped to the lowest since 1918, with only 130,188 visitors. With gas rationed, and men and women called to serve their country in the military and in war industries, Americans had neither the time nor the fuel to travel. Of the visitors who did come to the Park in 1943, 17,000 were servicemen, reflecting a role change for the Park from stay-cation site to a place offering respite from the war.

It was a lean time for managing the Park as well. Many Park Service employees, including superintendent David Canfield, left for military service. Working with a reduced budget, the remaining skeleton staff focused on keeping things together until the war was over. Because the war demanded so much of the country's resources, only essential Park activities continued. Construction projects, major maintenance, and tourism development were all put on hold.

Paradoxically, as overall Park attendance declined with the war, attendance at nature activities went up sixty percent. The nature interpretation and education programs, begun in the early 1930s, uncovered a huge public desire to experience and learn about the Park's natural history. The Park's first museum opened in 1931, in a rustic building adjacent to Park headquarters in Estes Park. Here visitors encountered a mounted bighorn ram and the heads of deer, elk, and even bison on the walls, as well as exhibits on geology and Native American history. But the public's thirst for information kept growing. Soon small museums opened at the Bear Lake ranger station and in a stone shelter cabin on Fall River Pass. By the summer of 1937, the Park completed the conversion of Moraine Lodge's former recreation hall to the Moraine Park Museum. Of the Park museums opened prior to World War II, it is the only one still in operation.

When the war ended and gas was no longer rationed, Americans returned to the Park in droves. By 1948, visitation had rocketed, surpassing 1 million for the first time. It has not fallen below that benchmark since.

At the beginning of the 1950s, American families, flush with post-war affluence, were ready to hit the road to visit their national parks like never before.

The Never Summer Range was added to Rocky in 1930 as part of a twenty-two-square-mile land acquisition by the National Park Service.

NPS photo by Russell Smith, courtesy of Rocky Mountain National Park Archives.

High in the Kawuneeche Valley, the mighty Colorado River begins as a small stream.
NPS photo by Ann Schonlau, courtesy of Rocky Mountain National Park Archives.

8

The Birthplace of Rivers

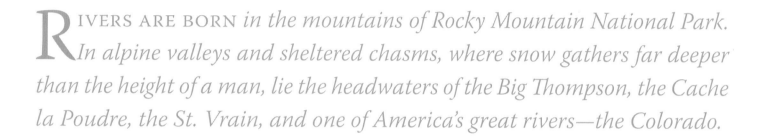

RIVERS ARE BORN *in the mountains of Rocky Mountain National Park. In alpine valleys and sheltered chasms, where snow gathers far deeper than the height of a man, lie the headwaters of the Big Thompson, the Cache la Poudre, the St. Vrain, and one of America's great rivers—the Colorado.*

The rivers of Rocky Mountain National Park flow either east to the Atlantic Ocean watershed or west to the Pacific, depending on which side of the Continental Divide they rise. The mountain snow that feeds them lies locked in deep layers and drifts until spring. Then lengthening days, warming temperatures, and the brilliant Colorado sun begin melting the snowpack, releasing the treasure of water downslope. Swelling like muscular water snakes, the Cache la Poudre, Big Thompson, and St. Vrain Rivers and their tributaries flow eastward to join the South Platte River, then on into the Missouri River, the Mississippi River, and eventually into the Gulf of Mexico. But Rocky's largest share of melting snow flows westward, carried by the Colorado River.

The Rivers

In the 1820s, so the legend goes, French fur trappers caught in a snowstorm buried, or "cached," their gunpowder along the Cache la Poudre River, giving the river its name, which means "hiding place of powder." Known locally as simply "the Poudre," the river descends 7,000 feet from its headwaters in the Never Summer Mountains in Rocky to its confluence with the South Platte River near Greeley, on Colorado's Eastern Plains. Seventy-five miles of the Poudre are

designated as part of the National Wild and Scenic River System, including fourteen miles within Rocky Mountain National Park.

The Big Thompson River begins in Forest Canyon and flows through Moraine Park to the town of Estes Park, where a dam across it creates Lake Estes. The North Fork of the Big Thompson begins in the

Within the Park's boundaries, the Cache la Poudre River meanders through meadows from its headwaters in the Never Summer Range.
NPS photo courtesy of Rocky Mountain National Park Archives.

Top: On a July 1976 evening, a severe thunderstorm dumped a foot of rain in four hours near the headwaters of the Big Thompson River, sending a twenty-foot wall of water down the canyon below the Park. Right: The flash flood washed out U.S. Highway 34 and inundated campgrounds, cabins, homes, and businesses.

NPS photos courtesy of Rocky Mountain National Park Archives.

Fed by the Roaring River at the Alluvial Fan, Fall River meanders through Horseshoe Park.
NPS photo courtesy of Rocky Mountain National Park Archives.

Mummy Range in Rocky and joins the main river in the Big Thompson Canyon. Fall River, which begins at Fall River Pass near the Alpine Visitor Center, is a tributary stream of the Big Thompson River. It flows into the main river at Lake Estes. From Estes Park, the Big Thompson begins a precipitous descent through the steep-walled Big Thompson Canyon, then across the skirts of the Front Range until it reaches its confluence with the South Platte, also near Greeley.

The Big Thompson often seems like a docile stream, shallow enough to wade across in many places, but it can swell into a raging torrent. An intense, nearly stationary thunderstorm on July 31, 1976, dumped twelve inches of rain in less than four hours over the upper reaches of the Big Thompson Canyon, just downstream from Estes Park. A 20-foot wall of water, flowing at more than 31,000 cubic feet per second, crashed down the canyon around 9 p.m., destroying cars, houses, and businesses, rerouting the river, and killing 143 people. This deadly flood occurred outside the boundaries of the national park.

The headwaters of North St. Vrain Creek, the north branch of the St. Vrain River, lie above Wild Basin along the Continental Divide. The St. Vrain flows into the South Platte River near Longmont, Colorado. It is named for frontier trader Ceran St. Vrain, who built a trading post along the river near its confluence with the Platte in the 1830s.

Critical to the history and development of the American West, the mighty Colorado River begins as a trickling mountain stream in the alpine valleys and high slopes of the Never Summer Mountains on the west side of Rocky. It flows through western Colorado into Utah, then through Arizona, Nevada, and California, then across Mexico's Baja Peninsula to the Gulf of California, dropping more than 10,000 feet in elevation over its 1,450-mile journey. Over millions of years, the Colorado River and its tributaries carved countless canyons across the American Southwest, including Glen Canyon and the Grand Canyon. Dams along it form Lake Powell and Lake Mead. Millions of Americans in those western states depend upon the Colorado for household, commercial, and agricultural water.

Preparing for his historic voyages down the Colorado River, iconic western explorer John Wesley Powell came to the Kawuneeche Valley in 1868 to reconnoiter the river's headwaters. Distracted by the looming summit of Longs Peak, he took a side trip to climb it, making the first recorded ascent of the mountain. Powell did not, it should be noted, float any part of the Colorado River through Rocky. He began his expeditions through what is now Canyonlands National Park in Utah, where the river is much larger, wider, and faster.

The Grand Ditch

In the decades after Powell's visit to the wild headwaters of the Colorado River, farms and towns mushroomed along Colorado's arid Front Range and Eastern Plains. In a region averaging only fifteen inches of precipitation a year, agriculture depended on irrigation, but stream flows fell far short of demand. Thirsty for water, the people of eastern Colorado saw plenty of it in the mountains, but it flowed the wrong direction for their needs. The solution lay in redirecting some of that flow.

Around 1889, the Larimer County Ditch Company undertook a grand scheme, the aptly named Grand Ditch. The plan was to build a series of ditches, canals, and reservoirs to capture water from the Colorado River, at that time known as the Grand River, and divert it toward La Poudre Pass on the Continental Divide. There it would be directed into the Cache la Poudre River where it could flow eastward to water farm fields in northeastern Colorado.

Redirecting a river is no easy task, especially without heavy machinery. And when the terrain is a roadless mountain wilderness at 10,000 feet, the job

A hiker walks the service road along the Grand Ditch high above the Kawuneeche Valley.
Photo courtesy of Grand Lake Historical Society.

In 2003, a 100-foot section of the Grand Ditch failed, sending a deluge of water down the mountainside.
Both photos courtesy of Grand Lake Historical Society.

becomes monumental. An army of workers armed with picks, shovels, wheelbarrows, dynamite, and pack burros journeyed high into the Never Summer Mountains in what would eventually be the northwest corner of Rocky Mountain National Park. Recruiting men for such hard work wasn't easy, and the company supplemented their workforce with Japanese laborers. American workers would not comingle with "foreigners," so the company built the Japanese a separate camp and brought in rice to feed them. Caves the men dug into the mountainsides to store their food and supplies are still visible near a back-country campsite in the area.

The men went to work with blasting powder, picks, and shovels, chiseling into the rocky ground. As early as 1890, the first water trickled eastward over La Poudre Pass. By 1894, the crews had completed three miles of ditch. Work continued intermittently through 1936.

By the early 1920s, it was evident that a reservoir was needed to contain and manage the additional water being diverted into the Cache la Poudre watershed. But the area was now within a national park, and it

took an act of Congress to remove land from within the Park boundary so that Long Draw Reservoir could be built.

Today the Grand Ditch is twenty feet wide and six feet deep, carrying water 14.3 miles to its terminus in Baker Gulch. It cuts across fifteen different high-altitude creeks, capturing and carrying an average of 20,000 acre-feet of water every year. The Grand Ditch relies on gravity to carry the water downhill to La Poudre Pass. The scar it makes across the eastern flank of the Never Summers is clearly visible from Trail Ridge Road, high up on the west side of the Kawuneeche Valley. The Grand Ditch is listed on the National Register of Historic Places.

Hikers in the Never Summer Mountains, thinking they're in a remote wilderness in the national park, are sometimes shocked to discover this man-made canal bordered by a gravel utility road its entire length. They even occasionally encounter a vehicle servicing the ditch.

In 2003, after more than a century of carrying mountain water, a 100-foot section of the ditch gave way, sending 105 cubic feet per second of water flooding down the mountainside into Lulu Creek and the Colorado River for several hours. The breach caused significant damage to wetlands, old-growth forests, and Park trails, and left a visible scar on the mountainside.

The Grand Ditch remains a controversial change within Rocky. Such an extensive, high-impact project would never gain approval today. By diverting between twenty to forty percent of the runoff from the Never Summer Mountains, it has a great effect on the ecology of those mountains and the Kawuneeche Valley below. Some people dislike the notion that the Grand Ditch manipulates the headwaters of one of the American West's great rivers. The National Park Service has fought in court to reduce the amount of water diverted by the ditch, and also to recover compensation for damage caused by the Grand Ditch breach.

Because the ditch predates the national park, and the water it carries is extremely valuable, it is one Park easement that is unlikely to be returned to nature.

Senator Adams' Tunnel

As the population in the eastern half of Colorado continued to grow in the early 20th century, so did demand for Western Slope water. As early as 1904, the U.S. Bureau of Reclamation outlined a plan for a tunnel under the Continental Divide to bring water from a large reservoir south of Grand Lake to the Eastern Slope, near Estes Park. Establishment of the national park in 1915 was supposed to halt any further water projects within the Park, but pressure mounted to build the water tunnel through (or under) Rocky. When a team employed by Weld and Larimer counties arrived in Grand Lake in 1934 to survey a route for the tunnel, chief ranger John McLaughlin blocked their entry into the Park. Undaunted, the engineers triangulated on the mountains from Grand Lake and from Estes Park, pinpointing locations for the east and west portals of a tunnel through Rocky without ever setting foot inside the Park.

In 1937, Colorado senator Alva B. Adams presented a bill before Congress to construct the tunnel.

Tunnel workers clear rubble after blasting in the Adams Tunnel, deep within Rocky's mountains.

Photo courtesy of Estes Park Museum.

After its thirteen-mile journey beneath the Park, Western Slope water sees daylight again at the East Portal, just south of Estes Park.

Photo by Mary Taylor Young.

Floodwaters from Lawn Lake widened the course of the Roaring River, hurling massive amounts of soil, boulders, broken trees, and other debris downstream.
NPS photos courtesy of Rocky Mountain National Park Archives.

"Not one inch of the surface of Rocky Mountain Park will be touched by this project," he assured detractors. Conservation groups such as the Izaak Walton League, the Wilderness Society, and the Colorado Forestry Association opposed the idea. So did the National Park Service, seeing the tunnel as contrary to the purpose and intention of a national park. But the political clout of Eastern Slope communities and farmers seeking water won the day.

On June 23, 1939, construction of the longest under-mountain water tunnel in the world began with the detonation of 144 sticks of dynamite at the tunnel's east portal. By August, a second crew began work from the west side. Over the next four years, except for a ten-month hiatus due to World War II, teams tunneled toward each other from both sides of the Divide at once. They worked round-the-clock in eight-hour shifts. In spite of the overwhelming nature of excavating thirteen miles through the spine of the Rocky Mountains, only one worker was killed, crushed by a railcar used to transport materials within the tunnel.

In a marvel of engineering planning, the two groups met deep beneath the mountains on June 14, 1944. When the tunnel was "holed through," the alignment of the two bores was off by a mere seven-sixteenths of an inch. Water was finally delivered through the Alva B. Adams Tunnel on June 23, 1947. True to the senator's promise, the east portal lies just outside the Park boundary, at the end of Highway 66 south of Estes Park. The west portal also lies outside the Park, on the east shores of Grand Lake next to the East Inlet trailhead.

The Adams Tunnel was only one piece of a massive water diversion plan known as the Colorado-Big Thompson Project, which was finally completed in 1954. While the Grand Ditch is a large-scale but low-tech project relying on gravity water flow, the Colorado-Big Thompson is a complicated feat of advanced engineering. It includes numerous reservoirs, pumping and diversion features, and sophisticated control of water flow. Today, Colorado River water is captured by Lake Granby (a reservoir), then pumped back to Shadow Mountain Lake (a reservoir), which was built to preserve the natural beauty of Grand Lake by regulating fluctuating water levels. From Shadow Mountain, the water flows into Grand Lake, then eastward through the Adams Tunnel beneath Rocky

Mountain National Park, through a second tunnel under Rams Horn Mountain to Marys Lake (a natural lake expanded by damming). It then passes through a third tunnel under Prospect Mountain to Lake Estes, a reservoir built along the Big Thompson River, which carries it downstream to thirsty users in northeastern Colorado. Whew!

The project can divert up to 310,000 acre-feet of water a year. Six hydroelectric plants within the project generate nearly 760 million kilowatt hours of electricity.

The Lawn Lake Flood

The Grand Ditch was not the only pre-national park water project in Rocky. At the park's founding, there were eighteen reservoirs and ditches within its boundaries. These included Bluebird, Pear, and Sandbeach Lakes in Wild Basin, which provided drinking water for Longmont, and Lawn Lake at the foot of the Mummy Range. The water rights for many of these projects were eventually purchased by the Park Service and the dams removed. But the Lawn Lake dam removed itself, to devastating effect.

Lawn Lake was a natural lake expanded in 1911 by construction of a dam across the Roaring River to hold drinking water for the city of Loveland. Just six years after the Big Thompson Flood killed 143 people in the Big Thompson Canyon, downstream from Rocky, Lawn Lake's earthen dam gave way. Around 6 a.m. on July 15, 1982, 220 million gallons of water crashed down the mountain, emptying the lake in about a minute. That much water, suddenly released on the mountainside, moved downhill with incredible force, carrying away everything in its path—dirt, rocks, trees, even boulders weighing as much as 450 tons.

When the water reached the valley of Horseshoe Park below, it spread out and slowed down. The rocks, soil, and debris settled out, creating a large alluvial fan that is still visible today. Though moving more slowly, the floodwaters killed three campers. Continuing down Fall River, the floodwaters took out Cascade Dam, adding the water it held to the deluge. Millions of gallons of water then rushed into the town of Estes Park, rising a foot or more within homes and stores and causing $31 million in damage. The flood was finally halted when the water entered Lake Estes.

When the Lawn Lake flood reached Horseshoe Park, the debris flow spread out, creating the large alluvial fan seen in the lower far right corner of this 1982 photograph of Horseshoe Park.
NPS photo courtesy of Rocky Mountain National Park Archives.

The Flood of 2013

At first, the rainstorm that began September 11, 2013, didn't seem unusual. But as torrential rains continued for days without letup—over Rocky and across the Front Range from Pikes Peak to the Wyoming state line—the rivers born within the national park swelled. Soon they would rage out of their banks with the waters of a thousand-year storm, wreaking devastation across 2,000 square miles and seventeen Colorado counties.

At the height of the storm, more than twelve inches of rain fell on Rocky in twenty-four hours. The Big Thompson River roared above flood stage for sixty hours, and the Roaring River carved a new path over the Alluvial Fan. Its raging waters joined Fall River, seriously damaging the Endovalley Road and Aspenglen Bridge, and overtopping the Cascade Dam near the Fall River entrance. Rain-saturated soils caused a large landslide on Twin Sisters Peak and swamped the Bighorn Ranger Station. Rising water damaged the McGraw Ranch bridge and road, Aspenglen and Longs Peak Campgrounds, and many trails, and inundated the town of Estes Park. The National Park Service evacuated Park campgrounds and assisted a few backcountry campers over flood-swollen creeks, but everyone got out safely. The flood

Swollen by the storm, the Roaring River cut a new channel in the Alluvial Fan, ·sawing its way through the Endovalley Road in the process.

NPS photo courtesy of Rocky Mountain National Park Archives.

Flooding damaged trails as well as roads, demolishing many footbridges in Rocky's back-country, including this one in Wild Basin.
NPS photo courtesy of Rocky Mountain National Park Archives.

forced temporary closure of Rocky except for essential travel over Trail Ridge Road, which for several days was the only road into or out of Estes Park as lower elevation highways flooded and were destroyed.

Days of heavy rain sent walls of water crashing down scenic canyons, flooding towns downstream and stranding hundreds. Tiny resort towns like Glen Haven and Drake were effectively wiped out. U.S. Highway 36 between Lyons and Estes Park was badly damaged by the North St. Vrain River. The Big Thompson River, in a terrifying replay of the 1976 flood, destroyed an estimated eighty-five percent of U.S. Highway 34 through Big Thompson Canyon. After an aerial reconnaissance as floodwaters were still raging, the Larimer County sheriff reported the canyon was "scoured down to bedrock."

The flood surge continued downstream, wreaking destruction across northeastern Colorado and into Nebraska. Nine people were killed (none in the national park), 6,000 people evacuated, 1,882 homes destroyed, more than 16,000 homes flooded, and 200 miles of state highways and 50 bridges damaged. With damages estimated at between $1.5 and $2 billion, the flood of 2013 would be second only to the 1965 flood of the South Platte River as Colorado's most costly natural disaster.

What led to this epic deluge? A warm, moisture-laden air mass moving into Colorado from the tropics bumped into the Front Range mountains and rose upward. Unable to hold as much moisture as it cooled and expanded, it released its wet cargo as torrential rain. Weak southwesterly winds and a cold front pushing down from Canada stalled the storm over the mountains, causing day after day of downpours. The stage was set for one of the most devastating floods in state history.

How much of a role climate change played in the storm is uncertain, but climatologists expect an increase in the frequency and intensity of storms, alternating with periods of extreme drought.

Floodwaters scoured stream-banks, rerouted some channels, and inundated many low-lying areas. Here, Fall River churns through the Alluvial Fan.

NPS photo courtesy of Rocky Mountain National Park Archives.

During the height of the storm, the Roaring River lived up to its name. The bridge at the Alluvial Fan became clogged with boulders, logs, and other debris, forcing the river to eventually cut a new channel.

NPS photo courtesy of Rocky Mountain National Park Archives.

Damage to roads on the Park's east side was extensive, including this washout along McGraw Ranch Road.

NPS photo courtesy of Rocky Mountain National Park Archives.

Even concrete bridges, such as this one at Aspenglen Campground, were no match for the full force of Fall River.
NPS photo courtesy of Rocky Mountain National Park Archives.

Flood relief was an interagency effort. National Park Service personnel rescued stranded people, helped clear mud from the streets in Estes Park, and pitched in to deliver emergency supplies to communities cut off by the flooding.
NPS photo courtesy of Rocky Mountain National Park Archives.

Still waters catch a reflection of Hallett Peak at sunrise.
Photo by John Fielder.

9

Money, Kids, and Cars: The 1950s and 1960s

T HE POWDER-BLUE STATION WAGON *with cat-eye headlights and tailfins maneuvered into the Bear Lake parking lot alongside dozens of other cars. The back doors flew open and out tumbled a boy in a red cowboy hat and two girls in pedal-pushers. "A chipmunk!" shouted the smaller girl, spotting a long-tailed animal scampering over the rocks.*

The kids dashed off. "Slow down," called Dad as he unloaded the ice chest. Soon the family was perched on a boulder overlooking the lake, munching on bologna sandwiches and sipping Coke from glass bottles. The youngest girl held out a Cracker Jack to another chipmunk.

"Say cheese," said Mom as she framed the family in the viewfinder of her Kodak Instamatic, trying to fit the shape of Hallett Peak into the shot. With a click she immortalized the family's summer vacation in Rocky Mountain National Park, an iconic record of American tourism in the 1960s.

When World War II ended, American GIs flooded home, eager to take up their lives as civilians. They went to college on the GI Bill, found jobs, got married, bought houses, and started families. In the decades after the war, Americans were affluent like never before. They had money, kids, and cars, and they were ready to hit the highway and visit their national parks.

Rocky Mountain National Park was right at the top of the list.

As soon as the war was over, visitation to Rocky boomed, increasing 160 percent between 1945 and

Hallett Peak enthralls visitors perched on the busy shores of Dream Lake on a summer day, 1954. In the 1950s and 1960s, people flocked to Rocky in ever-increasing numbers.
NPS photo courtesy of Rocky Mountain National Park Archives.

A ranger welcomes visitors at the Fall River Entrance Station, 1953.
NPS photo courtesy of Rocky Mountain National Park Archives.

1946. In 1948, visitation passed 1 million for the first time. It was the first sign of a coming tidal wave. In the 1950s, the national parks entered a period of unprecedented visitation. But the parks, including Rocky, were not ready for the boom. In 1956, Rocky had no visitor centers, few bathrooms, badly deteriorating roads and trails, and inadequate campgrounds. The Park had only two official picnic areas, each designed to serve twelve parties—hardly adequate to serve the needs of a million visitors!

A lone carload of visitors enjoys the view from Many Parks Curve on Trail Ridge Road in 1948.
NPS photo courtesy of Rocky Mountain National Park Archives.

By the mid-1950s, the parking lot at Many Parks Curve was a busy place.
NPS photo courtesy of Rocky Mountain National Park Archives.

Hidden Valley

The popular summer picnic site and winter sledding hill, Hidden Valley, was at one time one of the few commercial ski areas located within a national park. Locals had used the site since the 1930s, driving to the top of the valley along Trail Ridge Road, then skiing or tobogganing down through the trees. In December 1955, Hidden Valley Winter Use Area opened with two T-bar lifts and a ski lodge. A bus transported skiers to access alpine terrain above Trail Ridge Road. At its height in the 1970s, the ski area boasted two T-bars, two Poma lifts, and one double chairlift. The base lodge included a cafeteria, ski rental shop, and restrooms. But the idea of a ski area within a national park was always controversial. The site was prone to high winds and averaged only about twenty-four inches of snow in winter, leading to an accident rate that was two to four times the national average.

In its heyday during the mid-1970s, Hidden Valley kept five lifts running, including a double chairlift that followed the slender cut in the trees visible directly above the lodge.
NPS photo courtesy of Rocky Mountain National Park Archives.

Skiers at Hidden Valley, shown here in 1979, braved thin snowpack and often windy conditions.
NPS photo courtesy of Rocky Mountain National Park Archives.

Hidden Valley, which for a time was billed as Ski Estes Park, was closed to skiing in 1991. In the early 2000s, the Park Service removed the deteriorating lodge, lifts, and other vestiges of the development. With its slopes restored to native vegetation, and a network of walking paths and bridges over the creek, Hidden Valley is now a popular site for summer picnics and winter sledding and snowshoeing.

See the USA

See the USA in your Chevrolet. America is asking you to call! The automaker's advertising ditty said it all for American families in the 1950s. By 1960, eighty percent of American families owned a car. The building of the interstate highway system encouraged auto tourism but also changed the way people vacationed. Instead of going to one site and staying a week or more, post-war tourists spent only a night or two in one spot. So while the number of tourists increased, the length of their stay declined.

In Rocky, cars loaded with kids crowded Park roads. But these families wanted to visit on the fly, driving through the Park with only a few stops for a picnic, a bathroom break, or a snapshot at a scenic overlook. Then it was back in the car and on to another national park. To serve these on-the-go visitors, the Park shifted its focus to developing day use of the Park. Roadside picnic areas, campgrounds with drive-up campsites, short trails with interpretive signs, push-button recorded messages at pullouts, even a taped auto tour for the drive over Trail Ridge Road, gave visitors a quick feel of the Park that didn't require hours or days. This snapshot-style experience allowed the Park to host literally millions of visitors.

Mission 66

Floundering in a sea of visitation success throughout its system, the overwhelmed National Park Service

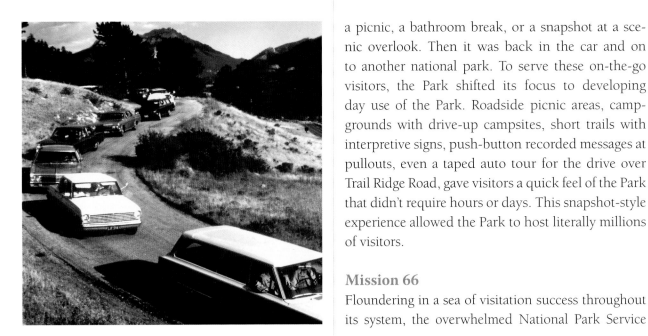

As Rocky's popularity boomed in the mid-20th century, Park roads saw a bumper crop of traffic.
Photo courtesy of Grand Lake Historical Society.

By the mid-1950s, a wide, well-graded Trail Ridge Road carried visitors to Rocky's alpine vistas.
NPS photo courtesy of Rocky Mountain National Park Archives.

devised a sweeping program to meet the needs of visitors. Mission 66 was a ten-year, nationwide initiative to update the national parks and expand facilities by the year 1966.

Mission 66 put the face on Rocky Mountain National Park that visitors see today. Prior to 1965, tourists had no orientation center where they could ask questions, view maps, and gather information for their visit. Limited information was available at Park headquarters in Estes Park, at the entry stations, at the Moraine Park Museum, and in a small exhibit room in the Fall River Pass store, but these places couldn't keep up with the demand.

In July 1965, a surprising new sight greeted travelers motoring up Trail Ridge Road—a low, modern building nestled on the tundra. It was built of stone and concrete, with clean, unadorned lines that fit unobtrusively into the landscape. The Alpine Visitor Center at Fall River Pass opened in 1965 as Rocky's first true visitor center, giving families driving Trail Ridge Road a place to stop to learn about the tundra, buy a souvenir, and get something to eat.

In 1967, the Beaver Meadows Visitor Center opened just outside the Park's new east entrance, which had been built in 1959. Now visitors had a place to learn about Rocky before entering it. They could study a relief map of the Park, get answers to their questions, pick up printed information on trails and wildlife, and watch an orientation film in the auditorium. The Kawuneeche Visitor Center opened in 1968 and provided similar services for visitors entering the west side of the Park. The three new

In 1967, the dedication ceremony for the new building housing Park headquarters and the Beaver Meadows Visitor Center marked the transition from the old, dilapidated Rocky to a modern park better equipped to serve its visitors.
NPS photo courtesy of Rocky Mountain National Park Archives.

visitor centers, products of Mission 66, were the linchpins of an improved Park, intended to help visitors understand Rocky and enjoy their visit like never before.

Mission 66 also added eighteen miles of new trails, improved and widened existing trails, updated roads and parking areas, reconfigured the Park entrances, built thirty-two modern comfort stations, installed two power-generating systems, and removed hundreds of old buildings and cabins. Modern administrative offices were included as a wing of the new Beaver Meadows Visitor Center, replacing the old headquarters building in Estes Park.

As the Park Service removed old lodges and resorts to restore the natural landscape, camping be-

What Is That Cabin?

More than seventy private cabins still lie within Rocky Mountain National Park, tucked into the forest or perched on the slopes around places like Moraine Park. Ownership dates from before the national park was created. Some of these cabins have been purchased by the Park but people continue to use them privately through leases. Terms of these leases vary, but many allow private use throughout the life of the seller, after which the property reverts fully to the Park. Other properties are still owned outright by private individuals. With rare exceptions, the Park buys inholdings under a "willing seller/ willing buyer" philosophy and rarely condemns property or forces a sale. Creative partnerships have been used to raise money to buy remnant inholdings, variously involving the Rocky Mountain Nature Association, The Nature Conservancy, land conservation trusts, or private conservation buyers. One day there may be no more of these private inholdings inside the Park, but that day is probably many years in the future.

came the only option for staying overnight in the Park. But Rocky's six campgrounds were already overwhelmed, accommodating twice the number of campers they were designed for. Mission 66 enlarged and modernized the campgrounds with loop roads, picnic tables, fireplaces, modern bathrooms with showers, and designated sites for groups. They built wider parking spots and installed hookups for camper-trailers. The amphitheaters were also enlarged to accommodate more evening programs and ranger walks and talks. To balance the loss of hotel rooms in Moraine Park, the Park Service built the Moraine Park Campground, the largest in Rocky. Park-wide, the number of campsites grew from 369 to 573 as a result of Mission 66.

By the early 1970s, $9 million of Mission 66 funds had been spent in Rocky Mountain National Park, transforming the dilapidated, overused Park into a modern, well-groomed national park that welcomed visitors.

The Changing Face of the Park

Present-day visitors see Rocky's rugged landscapes and teeming wildlife and think it's a pristine wilderness untouched by human hands. But a very different sight would have greeted them sixty years ago. Where elk graze on meadow grass in Moraine Park, they would have seen saddle horses and golf carts. Until the Mission 66 era, Moraine Park was a vacation paradise full of resorts, lodges, and summer cabins. There was a swimming pool, dancehall, riding stables, tennis courts, baseball diamond, grocery store, soda fountain, and even a post office.

Development wasn't limited to the larger valleys. Private lodges and cabins dotted the Park, even in areas that seem inaccessible. Today's visitors who hike on the Fern Lake Trail follow what was once the route to several hotels in the backcountry. The Forest Inn at The Pool and the Fern Lake Lodge at Fern Lake were accessible only on foot or horseback.

Returning the Park to a more natural state began in the 1930s with the Park Service's mandate for "removal of all fences and other evidence of man's handiwork." Between 1923 and 1963, more than 11,000 acres of inholdings were purchased and added to the Park. The impetus and funds of Mission 66 moved the process into high gear, razing 34 major lodges and re-

Bear Lake Road offers a glimpse of the Mummy Range, 1963.
NPS photo courtesy of Rocky Mountain National Park Archives.

sorts and 209 cabins. In 1932, there were 1,200 hotel beds within the Park. By 1963, there were zero.

The only surviving evidence of Moraine Park as a tourist mecca is a few inholding cabins and the Moraine Park Visitor Center, once the recreation hall of the Moraine Lodge. Nearby, the historic William Allen White cabin, former summer home of the

Cars fill the parking area at Sheep Lakes in Horseshoe Park.
Photo courtesy of Library of Congress (HAER COLO, 35-ESPK.V,4-8).

Fall River Road Redux

After its long-awaited construction in the 1920s as the first byway over the Continental Divide, Fall River Road quickly earned a reputation as a dangerous, difficult road. Once Trail Ridge Road opened in the mid-1930s, the Park Service closed Fall River. But after fifty years, public interest in the old road was growing. What secrets lay hidden along that storied route? What views awaited visitors after all those decades? Fall River was reopened in 1968 as a one-way road from Endovalley to the Alpine Visitor Center, offering a scenic circle trip for drivers to return down the Park's east side along Trail Ridge Road, or continue west to Grand Lake. Still unpaved, and with many sharp turns and steep inclines, Old Fall River Road as it is now called, remains a slow drive not for the faint-of-heart. But it offers a different view of the Park, and perhaps a small taste of early auto tourism in Rocky.

renowned journalist, is owned by the Park and houses resident artists every summer.

Rocky's Phantom Entrances

Tourists visiting the Park in 1930 could enter through a variety of gateways. From the west, they would have used a single entry point into the Kawuneeche Valley, just as visitors do today. But on the east side, they could choose from the familiar Fall River entrance, the High Drive along Deer Ridge, and an entrance off Highway 66 along the Big Thompson River. Once in the Park, the Big Thompson River entrance road came to a Y. The right-hand fork continued into Moraine Park. The left-hand fork passed through the YMCA camp into Glacier Basin, and then on to Bear Lake.

Visitors in 1930 wouldn't have had to pay an entrance fee. That didn't start until 1939, when the annual fee was $1 per car.

Through 1960, Fall River and Big Thompson remained the main eastern entrances. But the Big Thompson road was narrow, challenging to maintain, and plagued by blind curves. In 1956, the eastern edge of the Park was expanded with the addition of 320 acres. A new entrance road at Beaver Meadows opened in 1959 as the Park's main approach and site of the primary visitor center. Visitors continued to use the Big Thompson entrance until the cutoff road from Beaver Meadows to Bear Lake was completed in 1960. Today few people remember the phantom entrances to Rocky, but vestiges of the Big Thompson road are still visible on the slope above the trail between the YMCA camp and Moraine Park.

Architecture for a New Age

Along with the new approach to visitor use of the Park came a new style of architecture. Instead of the traditional log-and-stone buildings of the style known as Park Service Rustic, the new Park Service Modern architecture used industrial materials such as concrete, steel, glass, and plywood. The goal was for buildings to blend unobtrusively into the background instead of becoming landmarks of their own. Setting a design standard for new buildings meant structures throughout the Park would have a pleasing, uniform look instead of presenting a mishmash of styles.

The showpiece building for this new look was

the Beaver Meadows Visitor Center, set beneath the pines in the shadow of Longs Peak. Taliesin Associated Architects, comprised of former assistants and students of legendary architect Frank Lloyd Wright, designed the building with a light-filled public area to welcome visitors. For the building's frame they used weathering steel, which acquires a protective patina of rust that matches the reddish hues of ponderosa pines. Lichen-covered sandstone from a quarry in nearby Lyons softened the steel exterior, and the minimalist interior incorporated the outside with glass curtain walls.

As a hallmark of Park Service Modern architecture and the Mission 66 era, the Beaver Meadows Visitor Center was designated a National Historic Landmark in 2001.

Changes on the Horizon

By 1968, 2 million Americans a year were enjoying the updated Park. While the accomplishments of Mission 66 allowed Rocky to accommodate them, it also changed how they experienced the Park. Stop-look-and-go pullouts, visitor services clustered along roads, and a lack of lodging made Rocky a drive-through park. Few visitors got more than a superficial exposure or ventured into the backcountry.

But as the 1960s closed, America was entering a period of upheaval. Those kids who had sat on the boulder picnicking at Bear Lake came back as young adults eager to connect with the landscape. With the dawn of the 1970s, visitor interest in getting close to nature would bring a new set of challenges to Rocky.

Beaver Meadows Visitor Center, which also houses Park head-quarters, was designed by Taliesin Associated Architects to show-case the principles of Taliesin founder, Frank Lloyd Wright. The steel and stone building blends beautifully with its surroundings.
NPS photo courtesy of Rocky Mountain National Park Archives.

Storm clouds mass over Longs Peak.
Photo be Steve Mohlenkamp.

10

Treasures at Risk: The 1970s

A LINE OF HIKERS *inched toward the summit of Longs Peak along a vertical rock passage known as the Cables Route. Steel cables installed forty-five years earlier, in 1925, made this route up the North Face a challenging but nontechnical climb for hardy tourists.*

As afternoon clouds gathered above the summit, hikers in jeans and sneakers clogged the passage. Earlier hikers waited above for an opening so they could descend. "Among the best days that I have had outdoors are the two hundred and fifty-seven that were spent as a guide on Longs Peak," wrote Enos Mills a half century earlier. The hikers stacked up along the route or waiting above timberline as afternoon lightning storms gathered might not have agreed.

Loved to Death

By the latter half of the 20th century, Rocky had become one of the West's most popular national parks, passing 3 million visitors by 1978. But like a favorite teddy bear hugged too much, the park was suffering from the attention. The Mission 66 improvements had enhanced areas of the Park accessible from the road but done little to protect the Park's natural values and remote, wild areas. In fact, helping visitors enjoy this "outdoor museum" was increasingly in conflict with preserving it for future generations.

Visitors who had seen the Park through the windshield of the family Chevy as children in the 1950s and 1960s came back wanting to get out of the car and discover the Park's wild character. Longs Peak became a particular focus for more demanding, away-from-the-car exploration. In the mid-1950s, about 2,000 people a year reached the peak's summit. By the 1970s the figure was closer to 10,000. On an average summer day, 150 climbers hiked the route.

They weren't alone in wanting to get close to nature. Between 1965 and 1975, Rocky saw a 900 percent increase in backcountry use. But so many people hiking, camping, and exploring took a toll. Campers drove off-road into the backcountry, cutting tire ruts

Longs Peak and Rocky's other mountains are subject to sudden storms and the threat of lightning. Climbers often start their day at 3 a.m. so they can summit and be off the mountain well before afternoon thunderheads build.

NPS photo courtesy of Rocky Mountain National Park Archives.

Climbers pause for the camera on the north face of Longs Peak in 1927. Note the steel cable bolted into the rock; ranger Jack Moomaw oversaw its installation in 1925. The Park Service removed the cables in 1973, returning the route to its natural state.

NPS photo courtesy of Rocky Mountain National Park Archives.

Climbers on the summit of Longs Peak are well advised to be aware of those on the route below.

NPS photo courtesy of Rocky Mountain National Park Archives.

into the ground. Hikers trampled delicate tundra plants. Backpackers cut tree limbs for bedding and fuel, built fire rings, and dug trenches around their tents. Visitors loved their park but didn't know how to treat it gently and sustainably. "Man's impact must be minimized and controlled," concluded Rocky's 1976 master plan, to protect "this primitive core of a vast mountain region."

Fortunately, the huge increase in outdoor recreation and backcountry use in Rocky coincided with a growing national interest in the environment. By the 1970s, Americans wanted to preserve wilderness for its own values, not just as a playground for people. With the passage of environmental laws such as the Wilderness Act (1964), National Environmental Policy Act (1969), and Endangered Species Act (1973), the Park Service began hiring resource managers trained in plant ecology, wildlife biology, and environmental science, rather than just park rangers. Eventually, 249,339 acres (about ninety-five percent of the Park) would be designated as wilderness within the National Wilderness Preservation System.

By the 1960s, backcountry trail use was beginning to boom. Hikers on Flattop Mountain Trail walk in the footprints of the thousands preceding them.

NPS photo courtesy of Rocky Mountain National Park Archives.

Dwarfed by the rugged landscape, climbers on Longs Peak look like a line of ants below the Keyhole.
NPS photo courtesy of Rocky Mountain National Park Archives.

Protecting the Backcountry

To protect Rocky's wild landscape from being loved to death, the Park began making rules in the early 1970s for use of its backcountry. Backpackers could no longer camp wherever they wished. Before hitting the trail, they had to obtain a permit from the newly formed backcountry office, which also had maps, trail descriptions, and information. Camping was allowed only in a limited number of designated backcountry sites, with a maximum number of people and nights allowed at each site. To protect habitat and preserve a wilderness aesthetic, the campsites were situated away from streams and fragile areas, often tucked among trees or rocks to be less visible. Educating visitors to be good stewards of the land, Park managers encouraged Leave No Trace principles, urging campers to "pack it in/pack it out" and "take only pictures; leave only footprints."

Eventually, Park managers moderated backcountry rules a bit when they created cross-country zones. These allow hikers who are not traveling along established trails to camp where they want, provided it is at least seventy adult steps (about 200 feet) from

Hikers follow a path above the clouds on the tundra near Trail Ridge Road.
NPS photo courtesy of Rocky Mountain National Park Archives.

In this image from the 1920s, a park ranger surveys the serene surface of Chasm Lake. In the background looms the nearly 1,000-foot face of The Diamond, the massive east rampart of Longs Peak.

NPS photo courtesy of Rocky Mountain National Park Archives.

Climbing Straight Up

On any summer day, technical climbers can be seen scaling The Diamond—the nearly 1,000-foot wall of granite below the Longs Peak summit—like nimble spiders. Most climb the cracks and crevices of the peak's sheer East Face protected by ropes, but some "free solo," climbing without protection.

The rugged cliffs and summits of Rocky Mountain National Park have lured technical climbers and mountaineers for more than a century. In 1919, a Swiss mountaineer made the first technical ascent of Longs Peak. As climbing equipment and techniques improved in the latter 20th century, the number of visitors eager to go up the Park's rock walls boomed. The Diamond, one of the last unclimbed rock walls in the United States, was a particular object of desire. But concern for the safety of climbers, and those who might need to rescue them, led the Park to deem it off-limits.

In 1960, the Park finally allowed climbers to tackle The Diamond. To the chagrin of Colorado mountaineers, two climbers from California camped out at the ranger office to obtain the first permit and made the historic ascent. By the end of the 20th century, hundreds of technical climbers were scaling Longs Peak each year by various routes— a tiny number compared to the 20,000-plus hikers tramping the trail to the summit, but no small number considering climbers must sometimes cling to the cliffs by their fingers and toes. Climbers have named and plotted more than seventy-five climbing routes up the east face alone, with names like Ace of Diamonds, The Casual Route, and The Honeymoon is Over. Longs Peak overall has more climbing routes than any other prominent peak in North America and is among the continent's most popular and challenging mountains. Part of the attraction is its location near a major urban corridor. Climbers can work a full day at their job in Denver, be at their bivouac site by Friday night, and climb the mountain on Saturday.

To protect climbing areas and their fragile ecosystems from overuse, the Park began requiring climbers to obtain a bivouac permit to camp overnight. In addition to limiting a "bivie" group to no more than four, climbers are required to bivouac in the open, and only on rock or ice. The Park encourages "clean climbing," meaning techniques that don't chip or damage the rock such as installing bolts or pitons or chipping new holds.

A lone climber scales the massive vertical face of The Diamond on Longs Peak.
NPS photo courtesy of Rocky Mountain National Park Archives.

A climber plans his next move on the sheer face of The Diamond.
NPS photo courtesy of Rocky Mountain National Park Archives.

water and away from roads and trails. Campers must observe Leave No Trace principles and move their camp at least one mile every night.

Since the earliest days of tourism, visitors explored the Park on horseback. Some packed into the backcountry on their own horses, and others took pleasurable dude ranch trail rides or longer trips guided by outfitters. But decades of iron-shod hooves, droppings, and grazing left their mark: deeply gouged trails, collections of dried "horse apples," and invasive plants introduced from horse feed. In response, the Park closed many trails to horse or pack animal use. New rules allowed overnight camping only in specific stock animal campsites, banned any grazing, and required outfitters and horse packers to carry certified weed-free hay with them into the backcountry to prevent the introduction of exotic plants. Today, about 260 miles of trails in Rocky are open to horse use.

The cables on Longs Peak, increasingly seen as contrary to a natural experience of the Park, were removed in 1973. The Keyhole Route became the classic nontechnical path to the summit—still challenging but a climb that didn't usually require mountaineering equipment. Today, each summer

Although some trails are closed to stock use for resource protection, much of Rocky's trail system is open to pack stock, including horses, mules, and llamas.
NPS photo courtesy of Rocky Mountain National Park Archives.

Horses were a preferred mode of transportation within the Park in the 1920s.
NPS photo courtesy of Rocky Mountain National Park Archives.

May I Have the Envelope, Please . . . .

If you think Rocky's landscape is special, you're not alone. Beginning in the 1970s, the Park garnered numerous designations and protections.

The outstanding natural values of the Park's ecosystems, particularly the alpine tundra, led to its designation in 1977 as an International Biosphere Reserve by the United Nations. As the Rocky Mountain Biogeographic Province, the Park is part of an international network of protected ecosystems, recognized for its beauty and research value. Rocky's alpine tundra is an important indicator of such climatic changes as global warming and acid rain.

Portions of the Park are bisected by the Continental Divide. In 1978, those areas were designated as part of the Continental Divide National Scenic Trail, which traverses 3,100 miles from Canada to Mexico.

In 1986, the headwaters of the Cache la Poudre River within Rocky were designated a National Wild and Scenic River.

In 1996, Trail Ridge Road was named an All American Road and State Scenic Byway by the U.S. Department of Transportation.

In 2000, Rocky was designated as a Globally Important Bird Area by the National Audubon Society, recognizing its role in the conservation of numerous bird species.

In 2001, the Beaver Meadows Visitor Center was designated a National Historic Landmark.

In 2009, after years of effort by Colorado's congressional delegation, nearly 250,000 acres of Rocky Mountain National Park were designated as wilderness within the National Wilderness Preservation System. Only developed areas such as roads, campgrounds, and visitor centers are excluded.

Hikers on the Granite Pass Trail avoid wandering off-trail to protect fragile tundra plants.
NPS photo courtesy of Rocky Mountain National Park Archives.

The Tundra Communities Trail near Rock Cut on Trail Ridge Road affords visitors spectacular vistas as well as a close-up look at alpine vegetation while protecting the fragile ecosystem from overuse.
NPS photo courtesy of Rocky Mountain National Park Archives.

The Advent of Accessibility

The rugged mountain landscape of Rocky isn't easy for anyone to navigate but creates special challenges for visitors with disabilities. By the end of the 1970s, the Park had started to create ways for those visitors to have a meaningful experience of Rocky with an accessible trail around Sprague Lake. An adjacent backcountry campsite, named "HandiCamp," was constructed to be accessible by wheelchair along a half-mile trail. Today, the Sprague Lake Camp accommodates up to five wheelchair users. An interpretive boardwalk was built through the beaver ponds along Hidden Valley (since removed). The Park has a variety of trails and sites, ranging from marginally to fully accessible, built to accommodate visitors with disabilities. Federal law allows trained service dogs to accompany hearing- or sight-impaired visitors on any trail or campsite in the Park.

day, hundreds of hikers follow at least part of the Longs Peak Trail. The North Face, without cables, is the most popular technical route to the summit in winter and spring, and the fastest rappel back down in any season. Climbers sometimes clip into the old eyebolts, still anchored in the rock, which once supported the cables.

The Land above the Trees

For decades, visitors stopped along Trail Ridge Road to flock willy-nilly across the tundra, marveling at the endless view, the snowfields persisting into August, and the hardy plants surviving at the top of the world. But the alpine tundra wasn't hardy enough to survive the trampling of those thousands of feet. By 1970, alpine ecologist Bettie Willard wrote about the extensive damage done by uncontrolled tourism. "The activities of summer visitors to the tundra of Trail Ridge . . . results in the rapid destruction of vegetation in the areas seen by most visitors at close range—especially near parking areas . . . . Other activities affecting tundra are rock collecting, littering, crushing by car tires, and flower picking."

Walking across the tundra destroyed fragile alpine plants, compacted the soil, and exposed it to wind and water erosion. In a land of severe conditions and a short growing season, Willard warned, recovery might take hundreds of years.

Protecting the tundra became a priority. The Park began educating the public about this special ecosystem with brochures and interpretive signs. They directed visitors onto trails and designated some areas along Trail Ridge Road as Tundra Protection Areas, where no off-trail walking is allowed. Today, the paved Tundra Communities Trail near Rock Cut, with its series of interpretive signs, allows visitors to discover the alpine zone without hurting it.

The Bear Lake Boom

Nearly everyone who visits Rocky makes a stop at Bear Lake. This glacier-carved lake, with the magnificent forms of Longs and Hallett Peaks rising above it like rock stars, is the most visited site in the park. It's been a must-see since the earliest days, when the lodges and cabins of the Bear Lake Lodge crowded the shoreline. The iconic Cheley Western Camps began here in 1921 as the Bear Lake Trail School.

By the mid-1920s, Bear Lake's popularity led to crowds that were a foreshadowing of the future. "One day we'll have 50 cars a day coming up here!" complained Frank Cheley, who relocated his summer camp for youth outside Park boundaries in 1928.

As tourism boomed through the 1950s, 1960s, and 1970s, crowds and gridlock at Bear Lake became the norm. Traffic increased with construction of the Bear Lake cutoff road from Moraine Park during the Mission 66 years, which allowed easier travel within the Park. By the summer of 1974, more than 4,000 vehicles a day traveled the road.

Desperate to relieve parking and road congestion, the Park began a free shuttle system in 1978. The shuttle lessened road jams, but the visitors kept coming. Today, crowd-control features more typical of an urban park protect the lake from being loved to death, including buck-and-rail fencing, a paved path around the lake, and a ban on fishing. Even with these less-than-natural elements, Bear Lake remains a stunning scenic site accessible to all park visitors throughout the year.

Challenges to Come

Focus in the 1970s shifted from improving tourism to preserving nature, and Rocky Mountain National Park seemed back on track and aligned to its original mission. But in the last two decades of the 20th century, keeping the Park "natural" would bring challenges no one anticipated.

Well-worn trails are symptomatic of our love for the Park, but crowding, soil compaction, and erosion issues continue to challenge resource managers.
NPS photo by John Marino, courtesy of Rocky Mountain National Park Archives.

The Bear Lake area is often busy with visitors, and volunteers there help orient newcomers to their surroundings.
NPS photo courtesy of Rocky Mountain National Park Archives.

A bull elk keeps watch over his harem atop Trail Ridge.
Photo be Lee Kline.

Stewards of the Wild: Balancing Nature and People

O UR ELKS *(SIC)* ONLY LASTED *about three years. They came down from their high range just before Christmas, in 1875, by the thousands and were met by hunters with repeating rifles and four horse teams; hauled to Denver and sold for three or four cents per pound. In 1876, fewer came down; in 1877 very few were seen on this side of the Divide. In 1878 I killed my last elk, and to get him had to go over Flat Top.*

— Abner Sprague, *Estes Park Trail,* 1925

According to its enabling legislation, Rocky Mountain National Park was set aside "for the preservation of the natural conditions and scenic beauties thereof." But with constant changes in landscape, human use, and public attitudes, maintaining its "natural" character has been an ongoing challenge.

The Story of Elk
When the first settlers arrived in the area that would become Rocky, they found abundant wildlife. "One fall and winter," Milton Estes recalled in his memoir, "the writer killed one hundred head of elk, besides other game, such as mountain sheep, deer and antelope . . . by this time we had made a trail to Denver, where we sold many dressed skins and many hindquarters of deer, elk, and sheep."

As news spread of this hunting paradise, recreational and commercial hunters flocked to the area.

The wildlife seemed to be inexhaustible. But it wasn't.

By 1912 there were fewer than a dozen elk left in the Estes Park area. Faced with the loss of a major tourist attraction, local citizens purchased forty-nine elk to be imported to the area from Yellowstone and

Each fall, mature bull elk herd females into harems during the rut.
NPS photo by Ann Schonlau, courtesy of Rocky Mountain National Park Archives.

A bull elk bugles a challenge to any competing males.
NPS photo by Ann Schonlau, courtesy of Rocky Mountain National Park Archives.

Elk herds thrive in Rocky's lush meadows.
NPS photo by Ann Schonlau, courtesy of Rocky Mountain National Park Archives.

Coyotes, like this adult with four adolescent pups, are highly adaptable. They will eat whatever food they find or catch, including insects, berries, rabbits, mice, and carrion.

NPS photo by Ann Schonlau, courtesy of Rocky Mountain National Park Archives.

the National Elk Refuge at Jackson Hole. When the Park was established in 1915, the Park Service pitched in, actively managing wildlife in favor of "desirable" species. Though considered wrongheaded today, trapping and killing of predators such as wolves, coyotes, foxes, mountain lions, bobcats, lynx, and bears was standard practice at the time. By 1915, wolves had been extirpated from the Park, and by 1920 the last grizzly bear was gone. Meanwhile, the presence of "desirable" wildlife like elk and deer was encouraged. Park managers set salt licks near roads to draw elk and sheep, where they were more easily seen by tourists.

But managing in favor of the elk worked too well. Within a few decades the booming elk population overgrazed the meadows and stripped bark from aspen trees for food. They trampled willows and damaged stream banks. All of this had a negative impact on other species. Beaver, once so abundant that Abner Sprague trapped sixty of the "pesky animals" in Moraine Park one spring, were nearly eradicated on the east side of the Park because grazing elk destroyed the willows and aspen the beaver fed on. Elk also overgrazed alpine willows crucial to ptarmigan survival and pushed bighorn sheep onto marginal winter range. The peril of no more elk had become the predicament of a Park destroyed by too many elk.

In the 1940s and 1950s, culling the elk herd by shooting relieved the pressure somewhat, though it was inherently controversial. But in the early 1960s, the Park shifted to a "let nature take its course" policy. Managers thought that the elk would be limited naturally by available habitat. But as it turned out, nature's course resulted in the destruction of much of the Park's willow and aspen habitat.

In 1992, superintendent James Thompson wrote, "The biological vitality of the park is coming under significant pressure." Ten years later, the elk herd, still unchecked, had grown to between 2,800 and 3,400 animals in summer and about a third of that in winter. Willows were nearly gone along some streams, and many aspen stands were unhealthy and dying.

After years of study, planning, and public input, the Park instituted the Elk and Vegetation Management Plan in 2007, a twenty-year blueprint designed to maintain a summer population of 1,600 to 2,100 elk. It includes the culling of as many as 200 animals a year. Exclusion fences keep elk out of vulnerable aspen groves and willow habitat, giving vegetation a chance to regenerate. Maintaining elk in balance with the Park's greater ecosystem, while dealing with increasing pressures from a growing human population and impacts from climate change, will be an ongoing process.

Restoring Wildlife

Greenback Cutthroat Trout

"It only took a few minutes to catch all we could use as there were no small ones to throw back," wrote Abner Sprague about fishing in the Big Thompson River in the 1870s. Sprague was hooking greenback cutthroat trout, but if he'd fished the Big Thompson 100 years later, he wouldn't have caught even one of these native trout.

Greenback cutthroat trout, the Colorado state fish, was thought to be extinct by 1937, done in by overfishing and the stocking of more aggressive, non-native sport fish such as brown, brook, and rainbow trout. But the native trout weren't completely gone. People discovered a few remaining greenback cutthroats in a small stretch of a Park stream, leading to an extensive program to restore them in the 1970s. Listed as an endangered species at that time, greenback cutthroats now inhabit twenty-one lakes and nearly twenty-eight miles of stream in Rocky. Their status has been upgraded to threatened.

New research in 2012, however, muddied the waters on the greenback story. DNA evidence showed

Rocky's cutthroat trout are revered as aquatic art in motion by western anglers.
U.S. Fish and Wildlife Service photo courtesy of Continental Divide Research Learning Center and Rocky Mountain National Park Archives.

Restoration efforts in the 1970s restored greenback cutthroat trout to a handful of lakes and streams within the Park.
NPS photo courtesy of Rocky Mountain National Park Archives.

A young angler unhooks the trout on his line.
NPS photo courtesy of Rocky Mountain National Park Archives.

that the Park's trout aren't greenbacks after all but are likely a cutthroat species native to the Western Slope of Colorado, probably introduced over the last 100 years of fish stocking in the Park.

The new findings may lead to changes in how the Park's cutthroat trout are managed. Until then, the U.S. Fish and Wildlife Service still classifies them as the greenback species, and any of these trout caught by anglers must be returned to the water.

River Otters

River otters were absent from Rocky for decades, victims of intensive trapping for their fur. Between 1978 and 1984, forty-three otters from various states were released in the Kawuneeche Valley. Traveling along waterways, the otters dispersed through the west side of the Park and surrounding mountains, some moving as far as twenty-nine miles to establish a home range. The otter population in the Park fluctuates year to year, but averages a total of four animals.

Peregrine Falcons

Rocky was the first national park to restore peregrine falcons. The last wild pair known in the Park nested on the Twin Owls along Lumpy Ridge in 1959. Between 1978 and 1990, falcon chicks hatched in captivity were released in the Park. Today there is at least one active nest of this once-endangered species in Rocky.

Moose

It is likely that moose were never more than occasional Park visitors until their release in North Park by the Colorado Division of Wildlife in 1978. Able to

A cow and calf moose display the long legs and dense coats that make them so well adapted to winter in the mountains.
NPS photo by Russell Smith, courtesy of Rocky Mountain National Park Archives.

A moose calf rests in a day bed of wildflowers.
NPS photo courtesy of Rocky Mountain National Park Archives.

move long distances in search of habitat, moose soon took up residence in the Kawuneeche Valley, where they are now well-established. Moose are occasionally seen on the east side of the Park.

Wolves

Intensive efforts to eradicate wolves throughout the West led to their extirpation from Rocky, probably before the area was a national park. Despite frequent calls for the restoration of wolves to the Park, and their important role in a mountain ecosystem populated by elk, it is doubtful that managers will intentionally reintroduce the species. Wolves may eventually migrate into Rocky on their own from the greater Yellowstone region.

Boreal Toads

What happened to the toads? That was the question when biologists visited high-altitude lakes where boreal toads had once been common, and found none. Infection by a fungus seems to be the culprit that has led to the near extinction of this now-endangered

Velvet covers the antlers of a bull moose catching a snack on a Rocky evening.
NPS photo by Russell Smith, courtesy of Rocky Mountain National Park Archives.

While driving Rocky's roads, be alert for wildlife. Here, volunteers with the Bighorn Brigade direct traffic to ensure a ram's safe crossing in Horseshoe Park.
NPS photo by Beth Honea, courtesy of Rocky Mountain National Park Archives.

Boreal toads survive harsh conditions at high elevations that other amphibians cannot tolerate.
NPS photo courtesy of Rocky Mountain National Park Archives.

Researchers are hard at work reintroducing boreal toads to select sites in the Park.
NPS photo courtesy of Rocky Mountain National Park Archives.

During lambing season, some area trails are closed to hiking to reduce stress on bighorn ewes and lambs.
NPS photo courtesy of Rocky Mountain National Park Archives.

species. At one time, boreal toads bred in at least twenty ponds in Rocky, but over the years the species was reduced to five small breeding populations. Since 2007, Park biologists have released thousands of tadpoles, and some adults, at two additional sites. The tadpoles come from the state of Colorado's Native Aquatic Species Hatchery, where adult toads hatched from eggs previously collected in the Park are maintained as a captive breeding population. As of 2012, there was no evidence that the released toads had reproduced at the new sites in Rocky, but biologists are hopeful that populations will become established before reintroduction efforts end in 2017.

Balancing Recreation and Wildlife

Sometimes allowing wildlife to go about their lives means limiting the ways visitors enjoy the Park, especially during seasons when animals are raising their young.

Birds of prey, including golden eagles, peregrine and prairie falcons, red-tailed hawks, and great horned owls, find excellent places to nest on the Park's many rock faces, the same challenging cliffs that attract rock climbers. To protect raptors, some areas are closed to public use during the vulnerable nesting season. In March and April, when the birds are scouting for nest sites, most potential nest habitat is closed to climbers. As the birds choose their nest sites, areas not occupied by raptors are reopened to recreational use.

During the spring lambing season, the Crater Trail on the west side of Trail Ridge Road is closed to protect bighorn sheep. In Horseshoe Park, hillsides grazed by bighorn are closed to hiking, and volunteers of the Bighorn Brigade control traffic, allowing sheep to cross the road to reach a critical salt lick. The meadows of Horseshoe and Moraine parks are closed to people during the fall elk rut. Some Park lakes and streams are closed to fishing during the greenback cutthroat trout spawning season and to protect endangered boreal toads.

Keeping bears out of trouble is why all backcountry campers must now carry bear-resistant food-storage canisters and pack out all garbage and trash.

Young or old, black bears excel at climbing trees, using their claws and strong legs.

NPS photo by Ann Schonlau, courtesy of Rocky Mountain National Park Archives.

Rocky is home to about two dozen black bears, which can range in color from black to tan and cinnamon.

NPS photo by Ann Schonlau, courtesy of Rocky Mountain National Park Archives.

Native Plants

When work on Bear Lake Road ended in 2012, workers began restoring the disturbed roadside. Using plants that were tucked away in the Park's native plants greenhouse—grasses, wildflowers, and shrubs—they restored the roadway's natural appearance. But these weren't just plants from any old place. Before road construction began, volunteers collected seeds and dug up plants along the roadway. The plants were planted back where they were collected, thus maintaining the genetic integrity of Park vegetation.

Nursing native seeds and plants in Rocky isn't new. The CCC collected seeds in the 1930s, which they cultivated and planted in the Park to stabilize slopes, control erosion, and revegetate sites left bare by logging and overgrazing. In the 1980s, recognizing that plants collected at a site are the best ones to use to revegetate that site, the Park Service began focusing on ecological restoration using plants native to Rocky. The Park's first plant propagation area was no more than a fenced enclosure. Then workers built a homemade hothouse from old windows. In the mid-1990s, the Rocky Mountain Nature Association raised $70,000 to build an actual greenhouse in the Park. The 1,440-square-foot greenhouse is climate controlled, with Energy Star heaters and a thermal curtain that shields plants from the sun in summer and closes at night to hold in heat in winter. A special seed storage locker is humidity controlled and kept at 40 degrees Fahrenheit.

The greenhouse and nursery house 50,000 to 70,000 plants of 300 different species—from blue grama grass to columbines to aspen and limber pine. When trees must be removed in the Park to make way for construction or repairs, Park staff transplants any saplings up to three feet high rather than cut them down. Trees in the nursery include lodgepole, limber and ponderosa pine, and aspen, which will eventually be transplanted into campgrounds and areas devastated by pine beetles. When work is planned for the tundra, large blocks of turf are dug up and preserved in cold frames until they can be restored on-site.

In the greenhouse, volunteers germinate seeds in small trays and tend to seedlings. The "lives" of these plants are followed from cradle to grave. The date and place of collection and of re-planting are entered in a database. In this way, the life history of a particular wildflower growing in a specific site is known and can be monitored.

Rows of cinquefoil seedlings await their chance to bloom in Rocky's roadside meadows.
Photo by Mary Taylor Young.

Seedlings are pampered inside the climate-controlled greenhouse.
NPS photo by Ann Schonlau, courtesy of Rocky Mountain National Park Archives.

With Longs Peak in the background, Rocky's greenhouse gives native plant seedlings a head start on their mission to restore areas of the Park disturbed by construction, fire, or beetle infestation.
NPS photo by Peter Biddle, courtesy of Rocky Mountain National Park Archives.

Managing Wildfires

Stamp it out or let it burn? Over time, the approach to managing wildfires in the Park has changed. Through much of the 20th century, forest fires were put out as soon as possible. In the 1930s, the Park established fire lookouts at Twin Sisters, Shadow Mountain, the North Fork of the Big Thompson River, and near Longs Peak.

By the 1970s, the lack of fire as a natural force in the Park's ecosystem had produced dense, unhealthy forests, so the Park Service moved to a "let it burn" philosophy. Then a lightning strike in 1978 set off the infamous Ouzel Lake Fire. Wind gusts whipped it into a conflagration that threatened the town of Allenspark, and the National Park Service mobilized a force of firefighters. The 1,050-acre blaze was contained within the Park, but it showed that even the 266,000 acres of Rocky Mountain National Park are too small an area to safely allow forest fires to burn unchecked.

Today the Park Service uses prescribed fires—carefully planned periodic burns—to reduce the buildup of fuels in the Park's forests that might otherwise lead to a devastating wildfire. Dead and downed trees are manually removed in some areas, and natural fires are sometimes allowed to burn, carefully monitored, as a tool to improve forest health.

A firefighter on the 1978 Ouzel Lake Fire uses a shovel to smother flames with dirt.
NPS photo courtesy of Rocky Mountain National Park Archives.

The original fire lookout station atop Twin Sisters was tiny and extremely exposed. Severe thunderstorms must have played havoc with a fire observer's nerves.
Photo by E. P. Cole, 1916, courtesy of U.S. Geological Survey.

A helicopter with a bucket drops water on a hot spot during the Beaver Mountain Fire.
NPS photo by Ann Schonlau, courtesy of Rocky Mountain National Park Archives.

Little Beetle, Big Problem

Periodically, a creature the size of a grain of rice devastates the towering pines of the Park's forests, leaving large swaths of dead, brown-needled trees. The culprit is the mountain pine beetle, also called bark beetle, a native insect that has shaped western forests for thousands of years. Previous pine beetle outbreaks have affected Rocky Mountain National Park, but the infestation that began around 2007 is the most widespread and destructive to date.

These insects are a natural component of western coniferous forests, but recent warm winters and low precipitation weakened trees and favored the beetles, whose eggs and larvae are killed by very cold temperatures. More than a century of suppressing wildfires has also made forests unnaturally dense, with close-growing trees that make it easier for the insects to travel from tree to tree.

The adult insects burrow into tree bark and lay their eggs. The larvae then eat the living inner bark of the trees, eventually killing them. The trunks of infected trees are flecked with gobs of yellow sap known as pitch tubes, where the sap runs out of beetle bore holes. Various species of pine beetles attack lodgepole, ponderosa, and limber pines, Colorado blue and Engelmann spruce, and subalpine fir.

Not much can be done on a forest-wide level to fight beetle infestations, but high-value trees near buildings, campgrounds, and public areas can be treated with insecticide. Dead trees that present a hazard along trails and roads are removed.

Bark beetles are about the size of a grain of rice, but in numbers they can kill large swaths of western coniferous forests.
Photo courtesy of USDA Forest Service, Rocky Mountain Research Station.

Pine trees with brown needles— or no needles at all—are a sign that bark beetles have infested the forest. It's best to avoid areas with standing dead timber, especially during windy conditions.
NPS photo by John Marino, courtesy of Rocky Mountain National Park Archives.

Wildlife Within the Park

Black bears	20 to 24
Bighorn sheep	350+
Coyotes	Numerous
Deer	500 in winter (in Estes Valley); more in summer
Elk	600 to 800 in winter
Moose	30 to 50 on west side; uncommon on east side
Mountain lions	20 to 30 estimated

Trees that survive bark beetle infestation provide seed cones for the next generation, and the cycle of forest succession continues.
NPS photo by John Marino, courtesy of Rocky Mountain National Park Archives.

Morning alpenglow warms the ridge above Lake of the Clouds in the Never Summer Range.
Photo be Erik Stensland

12

An Outdoor Lab and Learning Place

H**IGH-PITCHED BARKS** *erupted across the rocks on the steep talus slope above Fall River Road. "There he is," said the biologist, pointing a directional microphone toward the source of the noise. The pika—a small mammal about the size of a guinea pig—blended so well into the rocks that only its scolding barks revealed its location.*

The University of Colorado researcher was studying the potential impacts of climate change on high-altitude species like pikas, which are uniquely adapted to live year-round above timberline. With more than 200 square miles of alpine tundra within its borders, Rocky Mountain National Park is an ideal "outdoor laboratory" for field research on this critical issue.

An Outdoor Lab

Research at Rocky has changed a good deal since the early days, when rangers rode out on horseback to count all the elk they could find. Or when measuring glacier expansion involved pounding an iron bar into a glacier, then returning the next year to see if the bar had moved downhill. *If* the bar could be found at all.

Today wildlife counts are made from the ground and the air, and population numbers are extrapolated using various methods and formulas. Glaciers are measured with sensitive technology, including satellite imagery. But these studies are just "the tip of the iceberg" when it comes to 21st-century research in Rocky. Highly specialized scientists who are experts in climatology, soil science, wildlife diseases, microscopic plant life, water chemistry, and many other disciplines make use of the unique landscape of Rocky to learn more about natural systems. With over a quarter-million acres of wilderness encompassing forests, lakes, high-altitude ecosystems, and an array of geologic formations, the Park is an outstanding outdoor research lab.

But it wasn't always viewed that way. Scientific

Denizens of rocky slopes at and above timberline, pikas use high-pitched barks to challenge intruders.
NPS photo by Ann Schonlau, courtesy of Rocky Mountain National Park Archives.

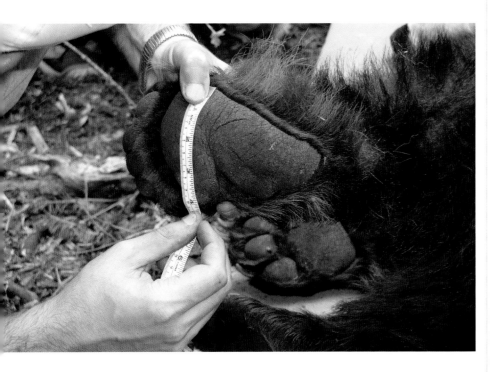

dealing with issues from wildlife to native plants to hydrology.

Rocky began to host a lot of professional scientific research after 1998, when Congress mandated that national parks make management decisions based on the highest quality science and information. They also required, and funded, a program to inventory and monitor natural resources in all the national parks.

Today, Rocky's research program is one of the most extensive in the national park system. Every year, the Park issues more than 100 permits for researchers from universities around the world, as well as from other federal and Colorado state agencies. Studies with titles like "Empirical Critical Loads of Atmospheric Nitrogen Deposition for Nutrient Enrichment of Mountain Lakes," may sound daunting, but they provide information of regional, national, or even global importance.

Measurements from a sedated black bear contribute to the wealth of data collected on Rocky's flora and fauna.
NPS photo courtesy of Rocky Mountain National Park Archives.

A researcher measures a dead aspen that offers habitat for cavity-nesting birds such as woodpeckers.
Photo courtesy of Rocky Mountain Bird Observatory.

Sample Studies: Pikas, Pines, and People

The study looking at the impacts of climate change on pikas, undertaken by University of Colorado researcher Dr. Liesl Erb, was the first to take a systematic look at pikas in the Park. Erb's findings, which found a link between increasing dryness, reduced precipitation, and decreases in pika populations, have important implications for pikas throughout North America.

Scientists also hope to find a way to preserve limber pine trees. They are studying white pine blister rust, a disease that has the potential to wipe out the Park's limber pines, which grow at timberline and are known for their dramatically gnarled, wind-sculpted shapes. In summer, volunteers fan out across the Park's high and remote forests to collect limber pine cones in hopes of finding individual trees that are resistant to blister rust. The seeds of these trees are maintained in the Park's seed bank. If the disease wipes out the Park's limber pines, these resistant seeds would be cultivated and then planted to restore limber pine forests.

studies were few and far between until the 1970s, when Park managers realized that managing wildlife and natural resources had to be based on sound science. In the 1980s, Rocky established a Resource Stewardship Division, with two employees who were professional environmental resource managers. These employees worked specifically on natural resource and science tasks, and had no traditional park ranger duties. Reflecting how greatly things have changed, the Resource Stewardship Division is now one of the largest in the Park, with eighty resource specialists

Lines of students walking slowly across the tundra, carefully scanning the ground, are part of another landmark study. The fifteen-year Systematic Archaeological Inventory Program has turned up some surprises about prehistoric, native people in Rocky. Conducted under the auspices of University of Northern Colorado anthropology professor Bob Brunswig, the inventory has found evidence of people in the Park dating back 11,000 years.

After the students finish their search, the open tundra behind them is dotted with small flags, each marking something a student noticed that might be evidence of ancient humans. Years of careful searching over some 30,000 acres have revealed ancient game drive walls, tepee rings, sacred sites, campsites, pottery fragments, and projectile points that originated from as far away as Yellowstone. For over 9,000 years, ancient hunters reused numerous sites, camping among the trees at timberline and hunting elk and bighorn sheep on the tundra. Analyzing how people have used this landscape over time also gives clues to changes in climate and the environment over thousands of years.

Researcher Above the Trees

It took only eight weeks in 1958 for tourists exploring the tundra from the new Forest Canyon Overlook along Trail Ridge Road to trample a path that destroyed up to ninety percent of the alpine cushion plants growing there. Many feet treading the same

Dr. Erb uses a special microphone to listen for pikas on a talus slope.
Photo by Mary Taylor Young.

Volunteers assist with important research projects in Rocky, including on-the-ground surveys of archaeological sites such as this tundra paleo camp.
NPS photo courtesy of Rocky Mountain National Park Archives.

Bettie Willard, shown here in 1961, painstakingly documented both Rocky's abundance of alpine plant communities and the damage from uncontrolled visitor use on the tundra.

NPS photo courtesy of Rocky Mountain National Park Archives.

ground not only killed plants but displaced rocks, compacted the soil, and led to erosion—damage that could take decades or centuries to heal.

Nobody paid much attention to how humans impact the tundra until Dr. Beatrice E. Willard came along. Scientists looked at the plants, animals, and ecology of the region, but Willard was the first to consider how tourists stopping along Trail Ridge Road and trekking across the fragile tundra damaged it. She constructed grids, then counted and classified every plant within the grid. "The amount of damage to plants decreased proportionally with the distance from the edge of the parking space," she wrote. She found that it took hundreds or thousands of years for a thin layer of organic soil to accumulate over the rocks of the tundra so that grasses and wildflowers could grow. Once disturbed, this thin crust took a very long time to regenerate. "It seems obvious that it is easier to prevent damage on the alpine tundra than repair it," she wrote in *Land Above the Trees,* a classic book on the natural history of the tundra, written with Ann Zwinger. First published in 1976, it is still

in print. "Where plants and animals grow at the outer limits of their existence, recovery is marginal and extremely slow."

Willard's landmark research, conducted at Rocky between 1958 and 1965, triggered Park managers to take action. The Park paved trails at Rock Cut, Forest Canyon Overlook, and Bear Lake; installed buck-and-rail fencing at Gore Range Overlook; designed a tundra-education trail at Rock Cut; and created a tundra etiquette policy describing how to travel on the tundra in areas of low visitation.

Willard first came to study Rocky's tundra as a field researcher for the Park Service-financed Alpine Wilderness Ecology Research project. She worked under the direction of Dr. John Marr of the University of Colorado Institute of Arctic and Alpine Research. Her study plots, established near Forest Canyon Overlook and the Rock Cut parking lot, are now listed on the National Register of Historic Places as the Beatrice Willard Alpine Tundra Research Plots.

Credited with creating awareness and protection for tundra worldwide, Dr. Willard studied and worked on alpine ecosystems for fifty years. She was the first woman named to the Council on Environmental Quality and founded the environmental sciences and engineering ecology program at the Colorado School of Mines.

A chance comment from the head of the Estes Park Chamber of Commerce on what could be done to compete with the town of Aspen for tourists led Willard to suggest a class on alpine ecology. That first class, offered in 1962, grew into the summer seminar series offered by the Rocky Mountain Nature Association, which celebrated its fiftieth year of continuous classes in 2012.

An iconic advocate for tundra landscapes and Rocky Mountain National Park, Bettie Willard died in 2003 at the age of seventy-eight.

The Rocky Mountain Nature Association

In the first decades of Rocky's existence, visitors flocked to enjoy its scenic wonders. The more they saw, the more they wanted to know about its plants, wildlife, geology, and history. But the Park administration had a small budget and more than enough to do managing hundreds of square miles of mountain wilderness.

ROCKY MOUNTAIN NATURE ASSOCIATION

www.rmna.org

Founded in 1931, the Rocky Mountain Nature Association plays a vital role in nature study and visitor education within the park.

Image courtesy of Rocky Mountain Nature Association.

In 1923, a dedicated group of citizens at Yosemite National Park formed an organization to support that Park's nature study and education efforts. A group of Estes Park citizens and business owners decided a similar "friends of Rocky" organization was needed. In July 1931, they founded the Rocky Mountain Nature Association (RMNA), with the help of Rocky's chief naturalist, Dorr Yeager. The group was one of the first national park cooperating organizations, predating the Yellowstone Association by two years.

RMNA quickly acted on its main goal of helping educate the public on the Park's natural treasures. By the next summer, RMNA produced its first publication, a fifty-seven-page, mimeographed brochure, *The Animals of Rocky Mountain National Park*. The humble publication was just the beginning of an extensive program that has supported the national park for more than eighty years. In the 21st century, RMNA's mission is still to promote the Park through education and interpretation; preserve and restore lands and historic sites within Rocky; and promote stewardship of Rocky and other public lands. The association has backed up its commitment with action. Since 1985, RMNA has raised close to $20 million and completed nearly fifty projects. A few highlights include construction of the Fall River Visitor Center, restoration of the William Allen White cabins and the Holzwarth and McGraw ranches, and construction of an accessible trail around Lily Lake.

Funded by the Rocky Mountain Nature Association, Fall River Visitor Center opened in 2000. It houses life-sized wildlife displays, a bookstore, and a discovery room where children can handle bighorn skulls and coyote pelts or try on a ranger uniform.
NPS photo by Debbie Biddle, courtesy of Rocky Mountain National Park Archives.

Exhibits at the Fall River Visitor Center encourage hands-on interaction.
NPS photo by John Marino, courtesy of Rocky Mountain National Park Archives.

Registration for each seminar is limited to 25 persons. The University of Colorado awards credit of one semester hour in upper division per seminar week, if the registration fee of $5.00 per week is paid **at the opening session** of each seminar attended. **Do not include registration fee** for credit with regular fees.

PLACE:
All seminars will meet at Hidden Valley Lodge in Rocky Mountain National Park. Field trips will be taken from there. No public transportation is available to and from Hidden Valley Lodge, nor are accommodations available there. Participants will pool transportation.

ACCOMMODATIONS:
Numerous hotels and motels are available in the town of Estes Park, 10 miles from Hidden Valley Lodge. Estes Park also has many restaurants, stores, and garages. Lists of accommodations will be sent upon receipt of your inquiry concerning the seminars.

Several campgrounds are available in the National Park within 7 to 11 miles of Hidden Valley Lodge.

Further information may be obtained by addressing your inquiry to the Executive Secretary of the Rocky Mountain Nature Association.

Alpine seminar participants examining tundra on Trail Ridge

Announcing

SUMMER SEMINARS
in
Rocky Mountain National Park

on

Plant Identification
Alpine Tundra Ecology
Mountain Ecology
Mountain Geology

ROCKY MOUNTAIN NATIONAL PARK presents an ideal outdoor laboratory for the observation and discussion of the identification and ecology of a wide variety of plants and animals, and of geology. Recognizing this fine opportunity for such studies, seminars in alpine and mountain ecology have been presented in the area and nearby for the past five summers. A seminar on identification of Rocky Mountain plants was added in 1965 and geology was added in 1966. All seminars are sponsored by the National Park Service, the Rocky Mountain Nature Association, the Institute of Arctic and Alpine Research and the Extension Division of the University of Colorado, the Conservation Education Division of the Colorado State Department of Education, the Estes Park Chamber of Commerce, and the Thorne Ecological Foundation.

In all seminars primary emphasis is placed upon field observations and discussion of the many facets of the landscape of Rocky Mountain National Park and adjoining areas. Previous participants have expressed appreciation for the benefits they have derived from the exchange of ideas and information among the members of the group, as well as for the formal instruction.

Each six-day seminar is held in Rocky Mountain National Park and its vicinity. The major portion of each day is spent in the field observing the various features of the landscape as it appears in this "living museum." Shorter indoor sessions follow each day's field activities, where field experiences are further discussed and illustrated. Distinguished scientists present evening lectures to complement the daytime activities.

A 1967 brochure from the Rocky Mountain Nature Association advertises its Summer Seminars on plant identification, alpine tundra ecology, mountain ecology, and mountain geology. Participants could get a semester hour's credit for each week through the University of Colorado.
Image courtesy of Rocky Mountain Nature Association.

RMNA operates bookstores in the Park's visitor centers and other locations in Colorado and Wyoming. Its publication arm has published twenty-six books and numerous newspapers, guides, and brochures. Its book titles range from the reissue of *Bob Flame, Rocky Mountain Ranger* to *Alpine Wildflowers* and *Rocky Mountain Rustic: Historic Buildings of the Rocky Mountain National Park Area*.

An Outdoor Classroom

Chief among RMNA's accomplishments is its education program. Rocky Mountain Field Seminars make use of the entire Park as an outdoor classroom. In a wide variety of classes ranging from hummingbirds and geology to tundra ecology and nature writing, visitors learn about and experience the Park. True to the name, seminars are largely conducted in the field.

The seminar program began with just one class. In the early 1960s, alpine ecologist Dr. Bettie Willard was often questioned by curious visitors while she was studying the tundra. Willard recognized not only that many visitors had a hunger to know more about the Park, but that this interest was an opportunity to enlist them as Park advocates and conservationists. Willard partnered with RMNA to offer a class on alpine tundra ecology in 1962. Fifty years later, in 2012, RMNA's Rocky Mountain Field Seminars offered 178 different classes, serving more than 2,200 people. Classes range from short, "discovery" outings for kids to weekend seminars for adults. Instructors include Park Service staff as well as recognized experts in diverse fields. The hallmark of each seminar is a hands-on learning experience in one of the most spectacular outdoor classrooms in the world.

Connecting to Kids

Rocky Mountain National Park stepped onto a national stage in the 1930s when the ears of the nation tuned in to NBC radio to hear a series of fifteen-minute broadcasts from Rocky called "Nature

Sketches." The broadcasts grew out of Rocky's Junior Nature School, one of the first national park programs for children.

In 1932, Park naturalist Raymond Gregg started the nature school by offering field trips and nature study programs for children ages seven to sixteen. He divided the older kids into boy Nature Scouts and Girl Naturalists. The school met at the Moraine Park Museum. Word of the nature school came to the attention of Denver radio station KOA, which arranged for national broadcast of the nature programs. In the 1930s version of "going viral," hundreds of teachers from all over the country tuned in, and then requested transcripts. The broadcasts continued through 1942, when wartime demands on radio time took precedence. Naturalist Gregg also left that year for military service, and the Junior Nature School faded.

After World War II, the Park revived a kids' nature program with the Bighorn Club, including a Chipmunk division for younger kids. It also established a Junior Museum with a workshop where children could work on crafts and projects. Connecting kids to nature was (and still is) an important part of Park interpretation.

In 1992, Rocky began a specific environmental education program tied to school curriculum. That year the Park hired a former high school teacher as an education specialist, the first such Park Service position in the Rocky Mountain Region. For over twenty years, the Park's education program has worked with hundreds of school groups that travel to the Park from throughout the Front Range and eastern Colorado. Through inquiry-based activities tied to state education standards, students explore the primary themes of the Park, including ecology, wildlife, plate tectonics, and glaciology. Schools offer their students field science opportunities, an experience that students can't get in the classroom. Kids benefit by getting out in the Park measuring, studying, and learning.

Preserving History and Nature

How do you preserve the Park's western history while also maintaining its natural values? Two historic ranches on the eastern edge of the Park prove it doesn't have to be one or the other.

Boys in the Junior Nature program crowd around a park ranger.
NPS photo courtesy of Rocky Mountain National Park Archives.

With a young audience at Bear Lake, a park ranger talks about geology, glaciation, fish, aquatic plants, the water cycle, and a host of other topics.
NPS photo courtesy of Rocky Mountain National Park Archives.

During a Junior Ranger program, children learn the differences between horns (keratin sheaths that are never shed) and antlers (specialized bony structures that are shed each year).
NPS photo by Debbie Biddle, courtesy of Rocky Mountain National Park Archives.

As a young woman, Ruth Ashton obtained her master's in botany from Colorado A & M, later Colorado State University. She continued her work as a field botanist after marrying Dr. Aven Nelson, a professor at the University of Wyoming and president of the Botanical Society of America. The couple collected plants throughout the Rockies, and also in Mount McKinley National Park in Alaska. Ruth passed away in 1987, age ninety, in Colorado Springs.
NPS photo courtesy of Rocky Mountain National Park Archives.

Plant Pioneer

Rocky's mountains and valleys have long attracted adventurers and artists, but it wasn't until the 1920s that botany student Ruth Ashton (later Nelson) made a detailed study of the Park's plants. Ashton worked summers as a front desk clerk at Rocky's headquarters. In her spare time, she tramped the Park, collecting and pressing dozens of plants, cataloging and identifying them for her master's degree in botany. In 1933 she published *The Plants of Rocky Mountain National Park*, a comprehensive guide for amateur botanists, which has been updated and reissued several times. In spite of Ashton's work and expertise, she was never appointed to an official position as a naturalist by the Park Service. She went on to work as a field botanist and occasional college lecturer and published numerous books on Rocky Mountain and western plants.

A Ranch for Research

McGraw Ranch, a historic cattle and guest ranch dating to the 1880s, was acquired by the Park Service between 1966 and 1988 as elk habitat. The original plan was to raze the ranch house and other buildings and restore the natural landscape. But a public outcry led to a compromise that preserved the historic buildings while using them to benefit the Park. A partnership between the National Park Service, Colorado State Historical Fund, National Trust for Historic Preservation, and the Rocky Mountain Nature Association raised $2 million to renovate the ranch's fifteen buildings.

Today the Continental Divide Research Learning Center at McGraw Ranch provides low-cost housing and work space for researchers who are conducting studies in the national park on topics as diverse as elk management and climate change. Fourteen researchers working on eight or nine projects—all living in the same facility—also create a scientific community. While they share meals and work space, they exchange ideas. A climatologist might offer new insight on a water quality study, or a glaciologist may have an idea for a pika researcher.

A biennial research conference makes sure that what happens in Rocky doesn't stay in Rocky. Once their work is completed, researchers share their results at the conference, making their studies more accessible to the academic community, Park staff, and the general public. This also enables new research to be considered in Park decision making.

A Ranch from the Past Protects the Future

Set against the stunning backdrop of Lumpy Ridge, the MacGregor Ranch was established in 1873, just a few years after Joel Estes "discovered" Estes Valley. Making a go of it ranching was never easy, but for decades Muriel MacGregor resisted pressure to sell out to developers. She maintained her family home as a working cattle ranch until her death in 1970, leaving it to the Muriel L. MacGregor Charitable Trust.

After Muriel's death, MacGregor Ranch and the story it has to tell of ranch life in the early days of Estes Valley might have disappeared beneath the tide of 21st-century tourism and residential development. But in the 1980s, Rocky Mountain National Park purchased a conservation easement on 1,221 acres of

Once a cattle and guest ranch, McGraw Ranch now houses the Continental Divide Research Learning Center, where scientists from a variety of disciplines can study and share ideas.

NPS photo by Peter Biddle, courtesy of Rocky Mountain National Park Archives.

Along with fourteen other buildings, the main house at McGraw Ranch was restored and modernized for research use by a partnership of public agencies.

NPS photo by Peter Biddle, courtesy of Rocky Mountain National Park Archives.

The MacGregor family, here in front of their home in 1893, ranched in Estes Park for three generations.

NPS photo courtesy of Rocky Mountain National Park Archives.

Today, MacGregor Ranch's historic character is preserved under a conservation easement. It continues as a working cattle ranch, with a living history museum open to the public.

NPS photo courtesy of Rocky Mountain National Park Archives.

the ranch to protect it from future development. The Park is responsible for ensuring that both the ranch's historic character and its natural landscape are preserved. In 2007, hiking access to Lumpy Ridge and Black Canyon was relocated away from the main ranch house. The site is a National Register Historic District and operates as a history museum open to the public.

Citizen Science

Each year, an army of knowledgeable people working in the field adds vast amounts of data and first-person sightings to the Park's base of scientific information. These citizen scientists—both volunteers and students—contribute thousands of hours to dozens of research projects. Dubbed "the Nerd Herd," they support professional researchers in the field in countless ways: gathering water samples, banding hummingbirds, counting and identifying plants, even collecting bighorn sheep droppings!

The Rocky Mountain Butterfly Project is probably the longest-running citizen science project undertaken at Rocky. Since 1995, volunteer butterfly chasers, particularly lead investigator Rich Bray, have monitored, studied, and identified the many varieties of these delicate, winged creatures that inhabit the Park. Under the guidance of Dr. Paul Opler of Colorado State University, butterfly volunteers make weekly counts of

Banding hummingbirds takes a steady, gentle hand. Researchers record information on each bird's species, sex, age, and weight.
NPS photo courtesy of Rocky Mountain National Park Archives.

Netting or collecting butterflies is not allowed in the Park, so the best way to "catch" one, such as this pine white butterfly, is with a camera.
NPS photo by Russell Smith, courtesy of Rocky Mountain National Park Archives.

Rocky is home to a wide range of butterflies, such as these Mormon fritillaries feeding on nectar from the bright yellow blooms of rock ragwort.
NPS photo by Karen Daugherty, courtesy of Rocky Mountain National Park Archives.

the butterflies they find within a specific five-meter-square area. Nearly two decades of scrutinizing butterflies has created a fount of information. To date, 140 species have been recorded within the Park, exceeding the statewide butterfly count for many other states. The list of names reads like poetry—dreamy duskywing, sleepy orange, painted lady, silver-spotted skipper, Southern dogface. Why so many butterflies in the Park? Researchers credit the diversity of Rocky's 6,700 vertical feet of various habitats spreading on both sides of the Continental Divide.

Though powered by volunteers, the project holds a research permit from the Park, which allows them to temporarily catch and then release butterflies. Collecting butterflies without a permit is not allowed in the Park.

BioBlitz

Ready. Set. Go . . . count every living thing out there!

Identifying as many plant, animal, or invertebrate species as possible in a given place over twenty-four hours is the goal of a BioBlitz. At Rocky, teams of volunteers, school kids, scientists, and others have gone into the field repeatedly on BioBlitzes since 2008 to inventory plants, animals, insects, fungi, and other organisms. They've counted beaver lodges, looked for birds, and collected water samples to check for tiny organisms.

In the decade leading up to the NPS Centennial in 2016, one national park a year hosts one of these special BioBlitzes. In 2012, Rocky was one of ten national parks chosen to host a *National Geographic* BioBlitz to celebrate the 100th anniversary of the National Park Service. The 2012 BioBlitz was part field science, part festival, and part outdoor classroom. Teams of school kids, families, and citizen scientists fanned out to study aquatic insects in Park waters. Then they gathered with the general public for a Biodiversity Festival, with exhibits, games, and entertainment, celebrating "Biodiversity is Everywhere." The results of the BioBlitz? The 150 scientists and 2,000 students and general public identified 489 species of plants and animals, from the massive to the microscopic, in Rocky Mountain National Park.

BioBlitz participants combine field work with intensive study to accurately inventory organisms in one given place over a twenty-four-hour period.
NPS photos by Peter Biddle, courtesy of Rocky Mountain National Park Archives.

Longs Peak frames the
still waters of Bear Lake.
Photo by Glenn Randall.

13

The Arts and Artists

"DAY DAWNED LONG BEFORE THE SUN ROSE, *pale and lemon colored. . . . From the chill, grey Peak above, from the everlasting snows, from the silvered pines, down through mountain ranges with their depths of Tyrian purple, we looked to where the Plains lay cold, in blue-grey, like a morning sea against a far horizon. Suddenly, as a dazzling streak at first, but enlarging rapidly into a dazzling sphere, the sun wheeled above the grey line, a light and glory as when it was first created."*

— Isabella Bird, *A Lady's Life in the Rocky Mountains,* describing sunrise on Longs Peak

Artists have captured the beauty and drama of Rocky since long before it was a park. Painters, writers, musicians, photographers, and other artists express for everyone the human experience of the Park and the emotions it inspires—joy, wonder, renewal, and at times, trepidation.

Photographers

Fred Payne Clatworthy, 1875–1953

An early 20th-century photographer whose photos of Rocky helped publicize the area, Fred Clatworthy found a way to live and work in the mountains by making a business of his art. He operated Ye Little Shop in Estes Park for thirty years, selling gifts, souvenirs, and his own scenic photos. Clatworthy documented dozens of scenes in Rocky Mountain National Park, becoming a nationally known landscape photographer who photographed for *National Geographic.* He was a pioneer in autochrome, an early color photography process that produced a color transparency on glass, and his landscapes were widely used to illustrate lectures on the mountain west.

The Front Range from Estes Park *by Fred Clatworthy showcases the photographer's sense of composition.*
Image courtesy of David Tanton.

William Henry Jackson, 1842–1943

Earliest among the artists to record impressions of Rocky was iconic photographer of the American West, William Henry Jackson. He previously photographed Yellowstone; his images were so dramatic they helped persuade Congress to declare the area a national park. Hired in 1873 to photograph landscape features being measured by the Hayden Survey, Jackson and his assistants hauled their cumbersome photographic equipment throughout a mountain wilderness that in forty years would be Rocky Mountain National Park. They captured stunning images of Black Canyon, Bear Lake, Gem Lake, Dream Lake, and other locations. Jackson scaled Longs Peak with other members of Hayden's party in September 1873, photographing many now-famous landmarks along the route, including the Boulderfield, the Keyhole, and the summit. Somehow the photographers managed to transport their glass photo plates, intact, out of the rugged mountains, preserving images of the Park from nearly a century and a half ago.

W. H. Jackson photographed these falls east of Grand Lake while with the Hayden Survey in 1874.

Photo by W. H. Jackson, courtesy of U.S. Geological Survey.

Painters and Printmakers

Albert Bierstadt, 1830–1902

Distinguished German-American artist Albert Bierstadt was among the first painters to capture the landscape of the Estes Valley. Bierstadt became enamored with the scenery and landforms of the West. He founded the Rocky Mountain School of landscape painting, a romantic style that is the western counterpart to the Hudson River School that dominated landscape painting in the mid-19th century.

Well-known from his massive paintings of western scenes in California's Yosemite Valley, he was commissioned by the Earl of Dunraven in 1876 to paint Longs Peak for the then-staggering sum of $15,000. His imposing canvas, eight feet wide and five feet high, is possibly the first professional painting of the mountain. *Long's Peak, Estes Park, Colorado* is rendered in romantic style, its flat summit and boxy top portrayed as sharply pointed, rising in snow-covered drama like a peak of the Himalayas. Though the painting hung for a time in Lord Dunraven's Irish castle, it is now part of the Western History Collection of the Denver Public Library.

Bierstadt also painted a quiet lake set on a forested moraine, which he called Whyte's Lake. The name of the lake was later changed to Bierstadt Lake. The moraine is named Bierstadt Moraine.

Richard H. Tallant, 1853–1934

Known as RH Tallant, this prominent landscape artist came to Rocky by way of Colorado's rip-roarin' mining camps, where he lived as a young man. Mainly self-taught, he painted frequently in areas that are now national parks, including Rocky, Grand Teton, and Grand Canyon. F. O. Stanley commissioned a number of paintings from him. An active commercial artist, his illustrations appeared in magazines and calendars. But he was also active in the Estes Park community, serving as a justice of the peace.

Charles Partridge Adams, 1858–1942

The Sketch Box was what Impressionist landscape artist Charles Partridge Adams called his Estes Park studio, which stood along Fish Creek Road, with stunning views of Longs Peak. Adams is one of Colorado's most noted landscape artists, adept at

Adams' brush deftly captured the play of light, as shown here in Moraine Park.
Image courtesy of Denver Art Museum.

Birger Sandzén's Mountain Lake *features stylistic similarities to the works of Van Gogh.*
Image courtesy of David Tanton.

capturing the luminous light of dramatic mountain vistas, whether in the fleeting moments of sunrise or sunset, or filtering through storm clouds or aspen. Adams moved to Estes in 1900, where he rented a cabin as a summer studio. "It was the simple life," he wrote later, "bracing air, beautiful scenery, flowering meadows, clear streams." He captured these elements in his work, sketching and painting hundreds of scenes

within what would become Rocky Mountain National Park. Adams worked primarily in oils and watercolors, his Impressionist style finding a large audience among visitors to the new national park.

Birger Sandzén, 1871–1954
Dubbed "the American Van Gogh," Swedish-American artist Birger Sandzén spent summers in the Estes Park area in the 1920s and 1930s. He captured many scenes of Rocky, primarily in oils, but also in watercolors and engravings. His paintings are known for strong brushwork, bold use of color, and for capturing the effects of light on the natural forms he painted. For more than fifty years, Sandzén was a professor at Bethany College in Lindsborg, Kansas, eventually becoming head of the art department. When the prestigious Babcock Galleries in New York scheduled an exhibition of his work, he turned down their offer to fly him in for the opening. "I am sorry," he replied. "I have classes and cannot leave."

Adma Green Kerr, 1878–1949

Trained at the Art Institute of Chicago, Adma Green Kerr was a well-known regional artist who made her home in Estes Park in the 1930s. Kerr painted mountain landscapes in oil and pastel, many commissioned through the Public Works Administration, which supported the arts during the Great Depression. Her paintings hung in numerous public buildings in Colorado, including in Rocky Mountain National Park. She had several group and one-woman shows at the Denver Art Museum and was a founding member of the Colorado Artists Guild.

Lyman Byxbe, 1886–1980

A one-man show at the Smithsonian Institute in 1937 garnered Estes Park printmaker Lyman Byxbe national recognition. Byxbe's primary media were etching, aquatint, and drypoint. Known for scenes of Rocky Mountain National Park and the Estes Park area, Byxbe's shop on Elkhorn Avenue also sold hand-colored photographic reproductions of his engravings to offer tourists a low-cost artistic souvenir of the national park. Byxbe developed a good business in "cabin portraits"—commissioned etchings of summer cabins, which were then printed as notecards and Christmas cards. As machine printing became more common, Byxbe prided himself on producing his work in the traditional fashion—inked by hand and printed one at a time, then titled and signed by the artist in pencil.

In the early days of the national park, dirt roads were single lane with few places to pass. When the scenery moved him, Byxbe stopped his car and sketched from the road while his wife walked back along the road with a flag to stop traffic, saying, "There's a little problem up ahead." Other motorists, thinking a rock slide had blocked the road, patiently waited until Byxbe gave the "all clear" signal, which really meant he had captured the scene to his satisfaction.

Dave Stirling, 1887–1971

Dave Stirling arrived in the Estes Valley in 1915. For fifty summers he lived and painted in the Park from his studio near Horseshoe Park, which he called Bugscuffle Ranch. Known for his colorful paintings of aspen, Stirling worked in oils on board.

Though trained at the Cummings Art School in Des

Lyman Byxbe captures the drama of Hallett Peak in this black-and-white print.
Image courtesy of David Tanton.

Dave Stirling shows his bold use of color in Indian Summer.
Image courtesy of David Tanton.

Moines, Iowa, and the Academy of Fine Arts in Chicago, Stirling enjoyed his persona as a western storyteller and yarn-spinner. He provided "local color" many summer evenings in the grand lodges that once stood within the boundaries of the national park, telling tales and plinking tunes on the piano. His western charm built a following among tourists who later visited his studio and bought his artwork.

Sculptors

Alexander Phimister Proctor, 1860–1950

Regarded as one of North America's finest Western sculptors of the early 20th century, Phimister Proctor spent much of his youth at his family's homestead cabin in Grand Lake. His years roaming and hunting the mountains on the Park's west side gave him an intimate familiarity with the landscape and the wildlife.

Proctor and painter C. P. Adams became friends and explored the mountains together, as the note on this 1883 image conveys, "Returning from a sketching trip in the Flattop Mts."
Image courtesy of Steve Andreas.

MY HOME IN THE ROCKY MOUNTAINS.

Isabella Bird's account of her time in the Rockies drew in readers with a blend of exciting adventures, splendid scenery, and mountain men with rustic charm.
Photo courtesy of Library of Congress (LC-USZ62-108524).

LAVA BEDS, LONG'S PEAK.

A page from A Lady's Life in the Rocky Mountains *shows Isabella Bird admiring the view from among lava boulders on the route to the summit of Longs Peak.*
Photo courtesy of Library of Congress (LC-USZ62-108523).

He painted and sketched scenes of the Park, but it was in his sculptures that he truly translated his knowledge of the mountains into artistic expression. He studied and sketched the animals he hunted, and his work is remarkable for its anatomical accuracy as well as its vitality. A contemporary of Frederic Remington and Charles M. Russell, Proctor is known for his monumental bronze statues. His *Broncho Buster* and *On the War Trail* sculptures stand in Denver's Civic Center, chosen because they embody the untamed frontier spirit of Colorado.

Writers

Isabella Bird, 1831–1904

In an era when women were expected to live quiet lives and stay tied to the home, middle-aged Englishwoman Isabella Bird traveled solo to Australia, Hawaii (then known as the Sandwich Islands), India, China, Korea, Japan, Singapore, Vietnam, and Morocco, and wrote vividly about her experiences. She is remembered today for her adventures in what would become Rocky Mountain National Park, which she published in 1879 as *A Lady's Life in the Rocky Mountains*.

Bird was an accomplished travel writer, widely read by her Victorian audience. In the fall of 1873, Bird arrived in Estes Park, still a wild mountain valley with only a few hardy inhabitants. She galloped on horseback through the long grass of the area, climbed to the summit of Longs Peak, and is rumored to have engaged in a romance with colorful local "Mountain Jim" Nugent. Bird wrote detailed letters to her sister back in England. *A Lady's Life* grew out of those letters, much of it first published in the British magazine *Leisure Hour*. Bird's vivid prose and lively writing captured the landscape and characters of her journeys.

In 1892, Bird became the first woman to be made a "fellow" of the Royal Geographical Society. Though Bird published thirteen books and many articles, it is her descriptions of the pristine mountain landscape now preserved as Rocky Mountain National Park that has kept *A Lady's Life* in continuous publication for nearly 140 years and made her a much-loved, iconic writer.

Enos Mills, 1870–1922

Often called the father of Rocky Mountain National Park for his passionate campaign to create the Park,

Mills heeded John Muir's advice to inspire popular support of conservation efforts through his writing. Mills eventually penned nearly twenty books on subjects ranging from the history of Estes Park to grizzly bears, birds, and other wildlife.
Photo by Mary Taylor Young.

Kansas newspaperman William Allen White was a friend to presidents and a prominent commentor on national issues.
Photo courtesy of Chris Walker and Emporia State.

William Allen White enjoys the view from his cabin in Moraine Park.
Photo courtesy of Chris Walker and Emporia State.

Enos Mills was also an accomplished writer and photographer. Following the lead of his mentor John Muir, Mills began to write articles and books about his favorite topic, nature. His first major book, *Wild Life on the Rockies,* garnered him national attention as a naturalist and outdoorsman in 1909. Though he had only an eighth-grade education, he published nearly twenty books in his lifetime, including *Adventures of a Nature Guide, Story of a Thousand-Year Pine,* and *Your National Parks.* His essays on the joys of nature and the importance of conservation appeared in many of the major periodicals of the day, including *Colliers, The Atlantic, Saturday Evening Post,* and *Boy's Life.* Mills also became an accomplished photographer, chronicling the stunning scenery and details of Rocky in dramatic black-and-white images.

Though Mills' turn-of-the-20th-century writing style seems quaint today, his prose brought the mountains vividly to life for countless readers across the country, enlisting public support for creation of the national park.

William Allen White, 1868–1944

Pulitzer Prize-winning writer William Allen White, owner and editor of the *Emporia* (Kansas) *Gazette,* first fell in love with Moraine Park on a college trip in 1889. He eventually purchased a one-bedroom, rustic cabin on the terminal moraine above the valley floor, with a million-dollar view of Longs Peak. For thirty years, White and his family spent summers at their cabin in Rocky as his reputation grew for being a small-town editor with his finger on the national pulse.

In 1896, White's editorial, "What's The Matter With Kansas?" criticizing the populist political movement, launched him to national prominence. Over the years, he hosted many important guests at the cabin, including governors, congressmen, and the likes of William Jennings Bryan, Clarence Darrow, and Jane Addams. He reportedly talked to President Franklin Roosevelt on his Moraine Park phone line—the conversation listened to by nosy, party-line neighbors.

The Whites built a smaller cabin behind their home to serve as a writing studio. Here White had a place to think and write, inspired by the scenery of Rocky Mountain National Park. He wrote many of his twenty-seven books, weekly editorials, and numerous magazine articles during his summers in Rocky. His editorial, "To An Anxious Friend," won a Pulitzer Prize in 1922. He garnered a second Pulitzer posthumously in 1947 for *The Autobiography of William Allen White,* which his son, "Young Bill," edited and published after his father's death.

William Allen White's creative legacy lives on in Rocky Mountain National Park. Bill White sold the cabin and its contents to the Park Service in 1972, and each summer it houses writers, painters, musicians, and other artists working in the Park as part of Rocky's Artist-in-Residence Program.

Other Prominent Artists

The landscape of Rocky has inspired many nationally famous artists through the years. Celebrated 19th-century landscape painter Thomas Moran came to the area with the Hayden Survey and sketched Longs Peak. Renowned photographer Ansel Adams photographed in the Park. Novelist James Michener brought Longs Peak and the Rocky Mountain National Park area into popular culture with his novel *Centennial*.

The Arts—Alive and Well in Rocky Mountain National Park

Ever since Thomas Moran's vivid paintings and William Henry Jackson's photos of Yellowstone helped build support for preserving that landscape, artists have brought enjoyment and appreciation of national parks to Americans who might never actually visit. Through the National Park Service's Artist-In-Residence (AIR)

Program, professional artists capture the scenic beauty and stories of the parks in their work. Currently, twenty-nine national parks have an Artist-In-Residence Program. Rocky's AIR Program, begun in 1984, is the oldest in the nation.

Each summer, Rocky hosts painters, sculptors, writers, composers, and other working artists who live in the historic William Allen White cabin in Moraine Park during a two-week residency. With a spectacular view of Longs Peak, the cabin is both home and studio where the resident artist works on a project and also creates an original work that is donated to the Park. The artist shares his or her work and artistic process through two public programs. Prospective artists from around the country apply in the fall and are selected by a panel of other professionals in their field.

Since the 1960s, the Rocky Mountain Nature Association's Summer Seminar Series has offered classes in the Park for both beginning and experienced artists. Taught by professionals, the classes in creative writing, poetry, watercolor, photography, and other disciplines use Rocky both as an outdoor studio and a place of inspiration.

William Allen White wrote prolifically from a studio above his cabin home in Moraine Park. The cabin now houses artists-in-residence while they ply their craft at Rocky.
Photo by Mary Taylor Young.

From a vantage high within the Park,
sunrise splits the eastern horizon.
Photo by Erik Stensland.

14

The Park's People:
Rangers, Volunteers, and Others

"WE LEFT THE INN BY THE LIGHT OF THE MOON. *Single file we plodded up the winding trail through the trees . . . . A red dawn blazed in the east above the distant plains. We moved silently and slowly and the sun was well into the sky when we reached timberline . . . about noon we reached Miss Vaille's body, which was at an elevation of a little over thirteen thousand feet. She was laying face downward on a large flat boulder with her arms partly extended, as though resting. We lashed four skis together, two skis wide, then lashed the body to them . . . . We picked our way down across the snow banks and frozen moors to timberline . . . . Another Longs Peak tragedy had been finished and written into the diaries of the rangers."*

— Jack Moomaw, *Recollections of a Rocky Mountain Ranger*

Rangers

In 1933, Park superintendent Edmund Rogers summarized the duties of a park ranger to include: " . . . protection of the Park's forests from fire, insects and trespassing; guidance, control and protection of the Park's visitors, maintenance and rationing of the shelter cabins; care and maintenance of public camp grounds; the keeping of detailed travel records and pertinent related data thereto; protection and control of the Park's wild life; preliminary maintenance of trails; and maintenance of the Park's telephone lines

Building trails is hard, physical work, a fact that hasn't changed much over the years. Here, trail builders use pick and shovel to create tread above timberline on the Longs Peak Trail.

Photo by W. T. Lee, July 22, 1916, courtesy of U.S. Geological Survey.

If the look on his face is anything to go by, Dixie McCracken thoroughly enjoyed his job as one of Rocky's first park rangers.
NPS photo courtesy of Rocky Mountain National Park Archives.

A park ranger's job duties are as varied as the day is long. Here, a ranger prepares a group to experience Rocky in winter on a snowshoe trek.
NPS photo by Ann Schonlau, courtesy of Rocky Mountain National Park Archives.

A ranger scans the horizon for smoke from Shadow Mountain lookout.
NPS photo courtesy of Rocky Mountain National Park Archives.

The nonchalance of the pipe in Jack Moomaw's mouth belies the energy he put into his work as one of Rocky's more colorful park rangers.
NPS photo courtesy of Rocky Mountain National Park Archives.

during the winter months as well as many other miscellaneous details during winter months and times of emergency."

Today the duties of a park ranger are much the same, with the important addition of helping visitors enjoy a great Park experience by providing interpretation of wildlife, wildflowers, history, and the scenery.

Rocky's first park rangers, Dixie McCracken, Frank Koenig, and Reed Higby, hit the ground running, fighting Rocky's first forest fire in September 1915, the same month the Park was dedicated. The early rangers built their own cabins and patrolled the Park's

350 square miles—on horseback in summer and skis and snowshoes in winter—all for $900 a year.

Jack Moomaw

In 1921, legendary ranger Jack Moomaw came to work at Rocky. Moomaw was a classic early 20th-century ranger. He rescued stranded hikers; searched for lost visitors; retrieved their bodies when they didn't make it back; chased poachers; made repairs to buildings, trails, and equipment; and tramped, rode, or skied over the Park's thousands of acres in all seasons. He helped bring back the body of climber Agnes Vaille in 1925 and subsequently installed cables up Longs Peak. When an extensive search for a boy lost along the Roaring River in 1940 failed to find any trace of him, Moomaw proved how hard such a search could be. He weighted a gunnysack with rags and rocks and threw it in the creek, where it was promptly swept below an overhang. Repeated dragging of that stretch of the creek failed to retrieve the sack.

Moomaw published his memories of twenty-three years as a park ranger in *Recollections of a Rocky Mountain Ranger.* His amusing stories leave the impression that he was smarter, hardier, and harder working than everyone else. Moomaw was opinionated and not shy about voicing his views on others, including women, co-workers, and bosses. Criticized for where he placed the cables on Longs Peak, he wrote, "If a clumsy person were to fall from where the cable was located, he could, at worst, be picked up in one piece. But if he fell from where those thrill-seekers wanted to put it, he would splatter." Moomaw Glacier is named for him.

Fred McLaren

Moomaw's counterpart on the west side of the Park in the 1920s, 1930s, and 1940s was the less-flamboyant but equally dedicated and hardworking Fred McLaren. At the time, each man was the sole full-time ranger on his side of the Park. McLaren served thirty-seven years as a park ranger, most of it at Rocky. Three of his sons followed him into the Park Service. "He was one of the best all-around mountain men I have ever known," Jack Moomaw wrote about McLaren. McLaren Hall, one of the Park's administrative buildings, is named for him.

Not only did ranger McLaren do the usual duties of park patrol, maintenance, trail work, rescue of hikers, apprehension of poachers, and wildlife management, he even helped investigate a murder. In 1926, the cabin of Grand Lake-area settler Fred Selak was ransacked, its owner nowhere to be found. Selak was also the McLaren family's closest neighbor along Pole Creek. Ranger McLaren helped the Grand County sheriff and detectives from Denver track down two men who were making purchases with rare coins owned by Selak. The culprits confessed to burglarizing the cabin, then led the investigators to a remote corner of the Park where Selak's body was still

Fred McLaren, shown here at the Grand Lake Entrance Station in 1936, served thirty-seven years in the National Park Service. Three of his sons also became park rangers.
NPS photo courtesy of Rocky Mountain National Park Archives.

Ranger Jim Detterline carries an injured hiker over rough terrain on Longs Peak.
Photo courtesy of Jim Detterline.

hanging from a tree. Convicted of murder, the killers were executed at the Colorado State Penitentiary.

Jim Detterline

Any visitor who climbed Longs Peak between 1984 and 2009 likely encountered Jim Detterline, who served for twenty of his twenty-five years at Rocky as a ranger assigned to Longs Peak. During those years, Detterline was involved in more than 1,200 rescues and numerous significant law enforcement incidents. He received the Medal of Valor from the Department of the Interior (only the fourth awarded in the history of the Park) for his role in rescuing two people stranded in Horseshoe Falls in 1995. He also managed to get struck by lightning three times while on Longs Peak. Undaunted, he climbed the peak for his 351st time in 2010, breaking a record of 350 ascents made by legendary guide Shep Husted, which had stood for more than 100 years.

In the Line of Duty

Backcountry ranger Jeff Christensen gathered his gear and headed out on a routine patrol on July 29, 2005. A strong hiker and experienced outdoorsman, Christensen planned to hike from the Chapin Pass trailhead through the Mummy Range and back out to the Lawn Lake trailhead.

When Christensen didn't return, the Park launched a massive search. For eight days, hundreds of searchers, twenty-five helicopters, and nine canine search-and-rescue teams scoured the area but found no sign of the missing ranger. Then hikers saw a body among some boulders below Ypsilon Mountain. Christensen had fallen and fractured his skull. His radio lay near him, and he'd wrapped a T-shirt around his head to staunch bleeding.

Jeff Christensen was the first ranger killed in the backcountry in Rocky. A plaque and bronze campaign hat set on boulders in front of the Beaver Meadows Visitor Center memorialize Christensen and his death in the line of duty.

Early Nature Guides

Rocky Mountain National Park licensed the nation's first female nature guides, Esther and Elizabeth Burnell, in 1917, with the caveat that their excursions be limited to day trips below timberline unless they were accompanied by a "first-class male guide." The Burnell sisters learned their craft at Enos Mills' Trail School at the Longs Peak Inn. Described as young ladies who were versed in flowers, birds, animals, and trees, they first had to pass a qualification exam. Elizabeth eventually also became the first female Longs Peak guide. The park superintendent reported that the girls were successful and popular.

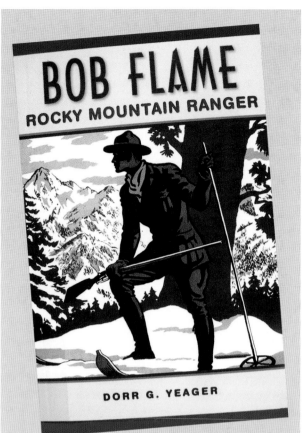

Legendary ranger Bob Flame brought adventures to life under the pen of Dorr Yeager, Rocky's first chief naturalist.
Photo by Mary Taylor Young.

Bob Flame!

As a ranger in Rocky in the 1930s, Bob Flame battled poachers, rescued stranded hikers, and protected the Park from various threats—but only from the pages of a book. The hero of a series of adventures in the national parks, fictional character Flame was the creation of Dorr Yeager, Rocky's first chief naturalist. First published in 1935, *Bob Flame, Rocky Mountain Ranger* gave a national audience a glimpse of life inside the national park while also teaching lessons of stewardship and responsibility. Yeager's square-jawed hero embodied the romantic ideal of a ranger, combining courage, resourcefulness, physical ability, and determination. The books helped fix in the public mind the image of a ranger as a hardy and courageous protector of nature, with a heck of an adventurous job!

Elizabeth Burnell guided in Rocky with her sister, Esther, who later married Enos Mills.
NPS photo courtesy of Rocky Mountain National Park Archives.

Dr. Margaret Fuller Boos was Rocky's first professional ranger-naturalist and one of only a few women rangers at the time.
NPS photo courtesy of Harpers Ferry Center (HPC-HFC/ROMO#58 1-2).

When he wasn't building museum exhibits or writing Bob Flame adventures, Dorr Yeager was out in the wild.
NPS photo courtesy of Rocky Mountain National Park Archives.

Enos Mills must have agreed, for he married Esther in 1918.

Margaret Fuller Boos

Dr. Margaret Fuller Boos headed up the Park's interpretive program during the summers of 1928 and 1929 as the Park's first professional ranger-naturalist. Boos, who held a doctorate in geology from the University of Chicago, led trips studying the Park's natural communities, attired like her male colleagues in high boots, breeches, white shirt and tie, and a Stetson hat. She gave public lectures at various hotels and lodges and edited the Park publication *Nature News Notes*. Public attendance at nature programming doubled during her stint. Dr. Boos went on to establish the geology department at the University of Denver in 1935, was department head until 1943, and also worked as a geological engineer. She conducted a sixty-year study of Rocky Mountain geology and established a scholarship at Northwestern University for women interested in geology.

Dorr Yeager

Rocky's first full-time park naturalist, Dorr Yeager, transferred from Yellowstone in 1931. Armed with degrees in botany, zoology, and philosophy, he set out to expand existing exhibits and museums, telling the Park's stories in the context of its landscape.

In 1932, he directed establishment of two museums, one in the Bear Lake Ranger Station and a second at Fall River Pass, in what had been a tundra shelter cabin. Next he oversaw conversion of a handsome log building that had been the recreation hall at the Moraine Lodge into the Moraine Park Museum. To educate visitors about Native American

Yeager was also a co-founder of the Rocky Mountain Nature Association in 1932.
NPS photo by Dorr Yeager, courtesy of Rocky Mountain National Park Archives.

history, he built a replica Arapaho campsite inside the museum, complete with meat-drying rack; travois; wood, bone, and hide artifacts; and a full-size, buffalo-skin te-pee. Upstairs, where large glass windows overlooked the glacier-carved valley, he fabricated exhibits telling the story of the Park's geology. But Yeager's efforts didn't stop at setting up museums. He organized lectures, field trips, auto tours, and self-guided nature walks. In 1931, he helped found the Rocky Mountain Nature Association and served as its first secretary (his father-in-law, Joe Mills, was the first president). He wrote the *Bob Flame* books, bringing the public stories about a courageous ranger who protected the Park for all Americans. Yeager later published books about North American wildlife and the national parks.

Though Yeager spent only four years at Rocky, he married Eleanor Mills, the daughter of popular Estes Park innkeeper Joe Mills (Enos' brother), cementing his place in area history both professionally and personally.

Ferrel Atkins

Digging deep into Park history and making it come alive for visitors was the passion and talent of long-time seasonal ranger, and later volunteer, Ferrel Atkins. Over more than thirty years as a summertime interpretive ranger, from 1952 to 1984, and then for nearly another thirty as a volunteer, Atkins' exhaustive research and detailed records earned him the title "historian of Rocky Mountain National Park." Dressed in a replica early Park Service uniform—green belted jacket, high leather boots, and campaign hat—Atkins delighted audiences with vivid stories of the lives and adventures of earlier Park visitors and inhabitants. He may be best remembered for his dramatic telling of the life of editor William Allen White, regaled from a rocker on the porch of the White summer cabin in Moraine Park. Atkins died in 2011 at the age of eighty-seven.

Wearing a replica early Park Service uniform, ranger Ferrel Atkins, shown here in 1977, regaled audiences with stories of the Park's history.
NPS photo courtesy of Rocky Mountain National Park Archives.

The NPS Volunteer logo incorporates the agency's iconic arrowhead symbol.
Image courtesy of the National Park Service.

Volunteers

Volunteering in the Park was a casual affair until creation of the Volunteers In Parks (VIP) program in 1970. VIP standardized volunteering throughout the National Park Service system, giving citizens meaningful opportunities to help preserve the nation's natural and cultural treasures. Through VIP, private citizens provide efforts without compensation that

Rocky's volunteers bring enthusiasm and expertise to the job, helping visitors have a "peak experience" whether on the trails, in a visitor center, or simply looking at a peak from afar.

NPS photo by Debbie Biddle, courtesy of Rocky Mountain National Park Archives.

Volunteer Tom Collingwood presents an interpretive program on native lifestyles at the Fall River Visitor Center.

NPS photo by John Marino, courtesy of Rocky Mountain National Park Archives.

Interpretive programs are often a highlight of many visitors' Park experience. Here, volunteer Maria Brandt prepares to talk about bats as part of the Junior Ranger program.

NPS photo by Peter Biddle, courtesy of Rocky Mountain National Park Archives.

With a little help from a volunteer, accurately identifying wildlife enriches a young man's visit to the Park.

NPS photo by Debbie Biddle, courtesy of Rocky Mountain National Park Archives.

are in addition and complementary to, but do not diminish, the responsibilities of park employees.

Today, more than 1,700 volunteers within 140 different job descriptions contribute 105,000 hours annually to Rocky. Their donated work is valued at $2.3 million. These volunteers staff information desks at the visitor centers, provide interpretive programming, and operate orientation points at Bear Lake, Longs Peak, and other sites in the Park. They assist professional researchers, help with citizen science studies, and act as caretakers for historic sites such as

McGraw Ranch and the William Allen White cabin. During the fall and winter breeding seasons for elk and bighorn sheep, volunteers of the Elk Bugle Corps and the Bighorn Brigade staff stations in Horseshoe Park. They answer questions and advise visitors how to view animals safely. The Nerd Herd volunteers help with research, studying bears, glaciers, butterflies, and many other topics.

One outstanding volunteer, Rich Bray, won the Enduring Service Award from the National Park Service for his more than 18,000 hours of volunteer help since 1995 on the Rocky Mountain Butterfly Project. Many volunteers have contributed 1,000 hours or more to the Park.

Rocky has had numerous longtime and colorful volunteers, including Walter Tishma, who began donating his time to the Park in 1988 at the age of sixty-five. He patrolled the Longs Peak Trail, offering advice to hikers and encouraging them in their quest to reach the summit. Between 1974 and 2000, Tishma himself reached the top of Longs 113 times, the last at the age of seventy-six. He passed away in December 2011.

Adventurers

Ladies on Longs

If Addie Alexander had climbed Longs Peak with the editor of the *Rocky Mountain News,* she might have been credited much earlier for being the first woman on record to reach the summit of Longs Peak. Instead, she was in a party led by Al Dunbar of Estes Park in 1871. She never wrote about her accomplishment, but her name was recorded within a rock monument on the summit and found later by another party. A mention also appeared in the *Boulder County News.* Little is known of this young woman, and it wasn't until the 1990s that she was given her due.

Alexander was outshone by Anna Dickinson, a prominent national lecturer who didn't reach the summit until 1873 but *did* make her ascent with William Byers, *Rocky Mountain News* editor, and the much-

publicized Hayden Survey. Long credited as the first woman atop Longs Peak, she is honored in the name of Mount Dickinson. Dickinson, however, was actually the third woman to climb the peak. Jane Bartlett climbed Longs a few weeks after Addie Alexander, according to a brief entry in the *Boulder County News.* All else about Bartlett's climb is lost to history.

Agnes Vaille

"Her features were those of one who was doomed," wrote Walter Kiener in later years of his climbing partner, Agnes Vaille, as they stood on the summit of Longs Peak in January 1925. Vaille's tragic death on Longs Peak is a cautionary tale of how even experienced mountaineers can be led to disaster by their passion and determination to triumph over the mountains.

Vaille was an experienced outdoorswoman and early member of the Colorado Mountain Club. She and Kiener, a Swiss mountaineer, set out on January 10, 1925, to make the first winter ascent of the east face of Longs Peak. They spent a cold, fitful night at the Timberline Cabin, a drafty structure built by Enos Mills in 1908. Setting out in bitter cold, they spent hours chopping steps in the snow and ice of

News of Agnes Vaille's death made headlines in Denver.

NPS photo courtesy of Rocky Mountain National Park Archives.

THE ROCKY MOUNT

AGNES VAILLE DIES IN STORM AFTER CLIMBING LONGS PEAK

Body of Chamber of Commerce Secretary Found Frozen in Snow.

(Continued From Page One.)

Oscar Brown; Jacob Christy and Herbert Sortland, all employed at the Inn. Sortland became exhausted after going about a mile from the house and, suffering from a frozen face and frozen ears, left the party and started back to the shelter. That was the last any of the party saw of the man and it is feared that he fell exhausted in the deep snow and froze to death. Thermometers carried by Kiener showed a temperature of 50 degrees below zero. The heavy snow storm, virtually a blizzard, which raged on the peak yesterday, was accompanied by a strong wind.

Body Found Frozen in Snow.

When the party of men reached the spot where Kiener had left his companion, they found her lying in the snow, dead from the cold and exposure. She had evidently succumbed to her desire for sleep, natural to one slowly freezing to death, and had died but a short time before her rescuers reached her. She had been alone on the mountain saddle from 11 o'clock yesterday morning to 4 o'clock yesterday afternoon, when the men found her body. Kiener's journey to the shelter house and the return trip of the party consuming this amount of time because of the severity of the storm.

AGNES W. VAILLE.

This 1927 photo shows the Agnes Wolcott Vaille Memorial Shelter at the Keyhole on Longs Peak shortly after it was completed.

NPS photo courtesy of Rocky Mountain National Park Archives.

the Notch Couloir. They finally reached the summit by about 4 a.m., the exhausted Vaille helped along by Kiener. The temperature was 14 degrees below zero, with fierce winds.

On the descent of the North Face, Vaille fell and tumbled 150 feet. She was unable to go on. Kiener, himself freezing and exhausted, continued alone for help. He returned with a party of rescuers from the Longs Peak Inn, but when they reached Vaille, she had died of exhaustion and hypothermia. Herbert Sortland, a rescuer who had turned back, lost his way and also perished. Kiener lost most of his toes and many fingers but lived until 1959.

Agnes Vaille was not the first person to die on Longs Peak, but she is probably the most well known. Her father erected a conical stone shelter in her honor in 1927, which still stands near the Keyhole. The Agnes Vaille shelter is on the National Register of Historic Places. The tragedy prompted Park superintendent Roger Toll, Agnes' cousin, to have ranger Jack Moomaw install steel cables along the North Face route where Agnes fell.

Michael Smithson

Loss of the use of his legs didn't stop Michael Smithson, a paraplegic interpretive ranger at Rocky, from climbing Longs Peak in the fall of 1986. Accompanied by two climbing partners, Smithson rode horseback to the Boulderfield. It took nine hours for him to lift and scoot himself across the rocks on a fiberglass seat, wearing out several pairs of gloves in the process. Then came two days of pulling himself up the mountain's North Face, using a system of three ropes—one around his waist as a belay, one his partners used to lift his legs, and a third an anchored handline he pulled himself along. Finally, after three laborious days, including two nights bivouacked on the mountain, the paralyzed climber reached the summit, having triumphed over an ascent that defeats many able-bodied hikers and climbers. Smithson went on to be the chief of resource education at Olympic National Park and retired in 2008 after thirty years with the Park Service.

George Hartzog

Rocky played a role in the career of legendary National Park Service director George Hartzog. From 1955 to 1957, Hartzog served as assistant superintendent of Rocky Mountain National Park. He went on to become National Park Service director from 1964 to 1972. Hartzog didn't sit idle while NPS director. He oversaw the acquisition of seventy-two new sites for parks, seashores, and historical monuments, including the first urban lands parks near New York City and San Francisco. Under his leadership, the National Park System more than doubled in size with the addition of nearly 50 million acres. Hartzog also guided creation of the Volunteers In Parks program. Park Service historian Robert M. Utley described Hartzog as "the greatest director in the history of the service."

As part of a three-man team (all coincidentally named Mike), interpretive ranger Michael Smithson summited Longs Peak in 1986, about eleven years after injuring his back and losing the use of both legs.
NPS photo courtesy of Rocky Mountain National Park Archives.

George Hartzog was assistant superintendent of Rocky from 1955 to 1957, then later served as the National Park Service director for eight years.
NPS photo courtesy of Rocky Mountain National Park Archives.

Viewed from the Emerald Lake Trail,
the Milky Way arcs over Longs Peak.
Photo by Glenn Randall.

15

Challenges for the 21st Century

"ONE HUNDRED YEARS AGO, *the Park superintendent was looking to run his little patch of the world. Today's superintendent must look at a broader landscape . . . . We aren't going to stop global issues like climate change here at Rocky Mountain National Park, so we must manage for them.*"

— Vaughn Baker, Superintendent, Rocky Mountain National Park

Through the ten decades of its existence, Rocky Mountain National Park has been a bastion of mountain wilderness, a place of renewal, recreation, and re-creation for visitors. Hosting more than 3 million visitors a year, it has grown to be the seventh most-visited national park west of the Mississippi. Over the years, the Park's history and management have reflected events and trends in American culture. When public attitudes about wildlife, wilderness, recreation, and cultural heritage changed, the Park responded.

As Rocky enters its second century, new challenges are already presenting themselves. Some of these are ever-present management issues that can be solved with sound policy and good ideas. But others may threaten the very existence of Rocky's natural treasures and the character of the Park as we know it.

Out of Room?

For 100 years, Rocky Mountain National Park has worked to be highly accessible to visitors, whether they want to hike into remote backcountry or drive across the Continental Divide. But that very accessibility may be one of Rocky's biggest challenges in years to come. With explosive growth along Colorado's

Front Range, Rocky is like an oasis of wilderness amid growing development, with more and more visitors flocking to the Park.

Balancing accessibility with overuse has always

One hundred years on, Rocky remains a haven for those seeking quiet solitude.
Photo by John Fielder.

been a challenge. Managing vehicle access, encouraging public transportation, and implementing a shuttle bus system are workable solutions that the Park has employed for many years. But how much is too much? Future managers may need to limit access during peak summer months when the Park reaches maximum visitor capacity. Park managers will have to determine what that number is. But making sure visitors have a quality experience will remain a Park priority.

The Next Generation and Beyond

"I came to Rocky as a kid, and fell in love with the mountains!" This is a familiar sentiment among older visitors, particularly Baby Boomers who visited as kids in the 1950s and 1960s. Many return to the Park in their later years, to work as volunteers or retire in the area.

But in the 21st century, the Park may not have as strong a following among young people. If Rocky doesn't make a connection with people while they are young, it risks being irrelevant in their adult lives.

Rocky must engage kids at a young age so they will be advocates for it, and all national parks, when they are voters and taxpayers.

Passing the stewardship of Rocky on to children is the goal of the Next Generation Fund (NGF). Created and administered by the Rocky Mountain Nature Association, the Park's nonprofit cooperating organization, NGF will be a permanent funding source for education programs at Rocky. In operation since 2006, the program is raising funds to meet its initial endowment goal of $10 million. Since projects, and federal funding, come and go, NGF will fill in the gaps when federal money falls short. Projects selected for funding must directly connect kids to nature in a measurable way. NGF projects will take advantage of the Park's greatest asset: the ability to inspire lifelong appreciation of nature by involving kids with highly trained educators, professional rangers, and programs tailored for today's (and tomorrow's) youth.

The Next Generation Fund is already supporting significant programming for kids and young people.

An American Conservation Corps crew uses a cross-cut saw and some elbow grease to clear a downed tree from one of Rocky's trails.
Photo courtesy of Rocky Mountain Nature Association.

The "Lily Lake Nature Hunt: A Virtual Geocache Adventure" is a popular outing for families. Named after a popular children's book, "Who Pooped in the Park?™" is a seminar for children that takes a fun and educational look at identifying animal scat and tracks. NGF also funds the Junior Ranger program and a Park newspaper just for kids. Reaching older students, NGF provides internships for college students who work with schoolchildren and the general public on projects for both RMNA and the national park.

Stewardship through Sweat Equity

How better to build future stewards than with the investment of sweat equity on worthwhile projects in a spectacular place? Living in the Park and working directly to improve and preserve it are the goals of two programs for older youth and young adults.

Shovels, mattocks, pry bars, and Pulaskis are the tools of the American Conservation Corps (ACC) trail brigades (not to be confused with the AmeriCorps service program). This NGF program brings crews of college students to the Park and nearby national forests every summer. The crews live in the Park and build new trails and repair old ones that have worn out or eroded. Begun with just one six-person crew in 2003, ACC has grown to four six-person crews. Participants are between eighteen and twenty-three years old and must be currently enrolled in college. During the course of their ACC service, participants learn about careers in natural resources, develop a sense of environmental stewardship, and directly improve the Park through on-the-ground construction work. Over the course of a summer, crews contribute 2,400 hours of service to public lands. Countless visitors have enjoyed Park trails built or improved by ACC crews, including trails to Mills, Dream, Emerald, and Cub Lakes, The Loch, Sky Pond, Lake Irene, and Storm Pass. Taking a break from trail duty, crews sometimes help with various plant and wildlife studies.

Engaging urban young people through physical labor in the Park is also the goal of the Rocky Mountain Green Team. This summer internship program (in partnership with Groundwork Denver) brings urban teens and young adults to the national park to work on Park improvement projects. The interns are mostly from low-income and minority populations. Many have never had a chance to

Researchers monitor airborne pollution at Lone Pine Lake.
Environmental Protection Agency photo by Dixon Landers, courtesy of Rocky Mountain National Park Archives.

visit the Park before. But when they join the Green Team, they hit the ground running—cutting beetle-kill trees, improving trails, and transplanting native plants to restore habitat. After a summer spent camping and working in the Park, the young people go home with a sense of pride and ownership. They know more about job possibilities in natural resources, and they've made a personal connection to nature and to Rocky. "Everybody worked real hard for ten-hour days. I mean we busted our butts out there and we did a really good job," reported one intern.

Fresh Mountain Air?

When they breathe the cool, clear air of Rocky, visitors don't expect to worry about air pollution. But the Park is downwind from many air pollution sources along Colorado's booming Front Range: power plants, factories, large farms, ranches, feedlots, and millions of cars. Fine particles from pollution and wildfires often create haze that clouds the Park's famous views. Ozone levels have been high enough at times for the Park to issue warnings against outdoor exercise. Mercury, pesticides, and other contaminants float into Rocky on air currents, then settle on water and plants.

Big Insight from Tiny Life

The high mountain lakes of Rocky Mountain National Park look pristine, like jewels of mountain wilderness. But when scientists test the waters, and the sediments at the bottom, they find an ominous story. The chemistry of the lakes has changed more in the last 50 years than in the previous 14,000.

How do scientists know what the lakes were like in 1960, much less 14,000 years ago? By taking samples of lake sediments that have accumulated over centuries, scientists gain important knowledge. In that pond-bottom muck are the remains of microscopic aquatic plants called diatoms. These single-celled algae have cell walls literally made of glass (silica), which do not decompose, so their remains accumulate and are preserved in pond sediment. Diatoms are also very sensitive to changes in water chemistry, making them good indicators of overall ecologic change.

Since the 1980s, researchers from the National Research Ecology Lab at Colorado State University and the U.S. Geological Survey have been studying the Loch Vale watershed, which includes Sky Pond, Lake of Glass, The Loch, and Icy Brook. When they examined sediment samples from these ponds—similar to studying the rings of a tree—they found that between 1950 and 1960 there was an abrupt increase in the number of diatoms that thrive when nitrogen builds up in the water. More diatoms means a lot more nitrogen. Increases were much greater in lakes on the east side of Rocky, near the Front Range urban corridor, than on the west side.

People who love the Park like to say that the mountains and forests of Rocky tell a story, if only we will listen. Paying attention to the ecological stories told by even the tiniest organisms of the Park may be the key to the future of Rocky as a whole.

One of the greatest concerns is the buildup of nitrogen, a major component of agricultural fertilizer. Nitrogen wafts into the Park in the air, then settles across forests, meadows, and lakes. As a result, grasses sometimes grow so thickly that they crowd out wildflowers. Nitrogen can also promote an explosive bloom of algae that takes over lake ecosystems. One of the grim possible scenarios of unchecked pollution is that lakes and streams become so changed by chemicals that fish can no longer live in them.

Air pollution problems can't be solved from just within Rocky, so the Park is working with the State of Colorado and the Environmental Protection Agency to monitor chemical changes, even in remote parts of the Park, and to formulate options for dealing with them.

A Changing Climate

Imagine Rocky Mountain National Park with trees blocking the vistas along Trail Ridge Road, with no snowfields or glaciers, no alpine wildflowers, and no unique, top-of-the-world animals like pikas or ptarmigan.

This could be the future as Rocky faces the greatest challenge in its history—climate change. The broad-ranging effects of a rapidly warming climate could alter the basic ecosystem of this high-altitude park. Some effects are already being seen. Spring snowmelt and runoff are beginning two weeks earlier, on average, than in the late 1970s. Drier conditions and

Freezing to Death from Global Warming

Warmer temperatures might seem like a good thing for wildlife trying to survive winter, but alpine-dwelling pikas are adapted for survival in the cold. They have thick fur and also rely on a deep snowpack to insulate them from extreme cold. If less snow falls, and that critical insulating snow layer melts too early in spring, pikas might use up their food reserves before temperatures are warm enough for them to survive. In a bizarre twist, global warming might cause pikas to freeze to death.

Red and yellow leg bands, applied by researchers, might be the only flaw in this white-tailed ptarmigan's remarkable camouflage.
NPS photo by Ann Schonlau, courtesy of Rocky Mountain National Park Archives.

warmer winters have favored pine beetles, leading to a devastating die-off of pine trees in the Park.

A symposium convened at Rocky in 2007 brought together climatologists, biologists, and other scientists to look at the range of possible impacts the Park might face from a changing climate and ways to start dealing with them. Here are some of the predictions:

- Temperatures will continue to rise, particularly in winter and early spring, increasing dryness and leading to earlier snowmelt.
- More precipitation will fall as rain instead of snow, reducing the snowpack and affecting water availability through all the seasons.
- More, and larger, wildfires will occur.
- Wetlands will shrink or dry up.
- As native plants die from lack of moisture, invasive plants will move in. Wildlife won't have enough food.
- New diseases, including West Nile virus, which are currently kept at bay by the Park's cold climate, could infect native plants and wildlife.

Rocky's alpine tundra, its crown jewel, is especially at risk. With warming temperatures, a longer growing season, and increased nitrogen acting as a fertilizer,

Pikas live at high elevation and do not hibernate. To survive the long, harsh winters, they must store enough forage during the growing season to last them till the coming spring.
NPS photo by Ann Schonlau, courtesy of Rocky Mountain National Park Archives.

lower-elevation plants and animals will expand upward and establish on the tundra. Grasses will crowd out alpine wildflowers, and trees will invade the tundra. While more grass will benefit elk, bighorn sheep will suffer from the loss of open alpine landscape.

As new plant and animal species encroach, there will be less food for alpine dwellers. Permafrost (perpetually frozen soil) will thaw, increasing stream flows for the short term but ultimately leading to further drying of the tundra and the loss of alpine plants.

Alpine specialists like pikas and ptarmigan, so wonderfully adapted to high-altitude life, won't be able to adapt quickly enough to the changes. Already living at the top of the world, they have no higher altitude habitat to move into and could eventually die out.

Hotter summer temperatures could force thick-furred pikas to seek shelter during the day. Hiding from the heat, they wouldn't be able to gather and store the food they need to survive winter. Encroaching wildlife would compete with them for food, destroy their habitat, and prey on them directly. Even the rocky talus slopes where pikas live might collapse as the permafrost beneath thaws.

Likewise, changing vegetation and invading wildlife may destroy or degrade the alpine willows that white-tailed ptarmigan depend on. With more and new species on the tundra, the ground nests of these birds could be trampled and their eggs and chicks devoured by predators.

Adapted to cold conditions and a short growing season, plants of the alpine tundra may not tolerate a warmer climate. Studies at the Rocky Mountain Biological Laboratory found that higher temperatures slowed the growth of mountain wildflowers. A defining characteristic of the alpine tundra is its lack of trees, but a longer growing season would allow trees to invade upslope. Scientists predict that a temperature increase of 9 to 11 degrees would eventually wipe out the Park's tundra ecosystem.

Faced with this complex network of potential problems, the Park is working to develop steps to deal with it. Collecting good baseline scientific information on temperature, precipitation, permafrost, hydrology, native plants, and wildlife, particularly pikas and ptarmigan, is the first step. In 2009, a Global Observation and Research Initiative in Alpine Environments site was established within Rocky to collect data specific to alpine habitats.

Climate change cannot be stopped, but developing strategies to deal with its effects may help preserve Rocky's unique landscape and character.

The Next 100 Years

What does the future hold for Rocky Mountain National Park? Plenty of challenges, certainly. But if history is any indication, we have reason to hope that the same energy and commitment that led to the Park's establishment a century ago will aid today's Americans in their effort to protect and preserve this special place, and its treasures, for another 100 years.

Melting Much Faster Than a Glacial Pace

Over thousands of years, the glaciers within Rocky have repeatedly grown and shrunk in response to environmental change. Massive ice age glaciers once filled Moraine and Horseshoe parks, but retreated as the climate warmed. Glaciers grew again during the Little Ice Age, a cold period from the 1500s to mid-1800s. Temperatures warmed again, shrinking Rocky's glaciers to their smallest recorded size during the mid-1940s. Cooler summer temperatures through the 1980s caused the glaciers to once again expand. Since the 1990s, summer temperatures have increased at such a rapid rate that many of the Park's glaciers are now smaller than their historic minimum from the 1940s. With overall climate warming, the future of Rocky's glaciers is uncertain.

Even protected as a national park, change is continual at Rocky. One constant is visitors young and old who thrill to the Park's vistas, wildlife, and history.
NPS photo by Peter Biddle, courtesy of Rocky Mountain National Park Archives.

As it has for a century, Rocky will continue to welcome adventurers of all ages.
NPS photo by John Marino, courtesy of Rocky Mountain National Park Archives.

Supremely adapted to Rocky's rugged environment, and as the main characters in a conservation success story, bighorn sheep are a fitting symbol of the Park's natural heritage.
NPS photo by Ann Schonlau, courtesy of Rocky Mountain National Park Archives.

Rocky Time Line

A Chronology of Events

1.5 Billion Years Ago

Tectonic plates collide, gradually compressing ancient sea sediments into schist and gneiss, forming what will become Rocky's oldest rocks.

Magma intrudes and cools, forming Rocky's granite bedrock.

140 Million Years Ago

The inland Cretaceous Sea covers the Park, and dinosaurs roam the shorelines.

80 to 70 Million Years Ago

During the Laramide Orogeny, the Pacific tectonic plate slides beneath the North American plate, uplifting the Rocky Mountains.

10 Million Years Ago

Another period of tectonic activity uplifts Colorado and parts of Kansas and Utah more than a mile. Longs Peak and other mountains rise even higher along fault lines.

29 to 24 Million Years Ago

Volcanoes bulge and erupt, forming the Never Summer Range.

2 to 1.6 Million Years Ago

Glaciers scour the Rockies, sculpting peaks and dredging valleys.

30,000 to 12,000 Years Ago

During the Pinedale Glaciation, glaciers fill Rocky's valley's with ice up to 1,500 feet thick.

11,000 Years Ago

As the climate warms and glaciers recede, Paleo-Indians begin crossing the mountains to hunt mammoth and bison on the plains. They camp near timberline, leaving evidence of their passing in the form of rock hearths, stone spear points, and rock walls used to drive game.

1200s to Early 1600s

Bands of Utes enter the future Park. By the 1700s, they have acquired horses and begin adopting a Plains Indian lifestyle, living in tepees and hunting bison.

1700s

In the late 1700s, the Arapaho, traveling from the northern Great Plains, arrive on the Colorado prairie east of the Front Range. As they enter the mountains in search of game, territorial skirmishes between Utes and Arapahos ensue.

Euro-American fur trappers and mountain men begin exploring the area, following rivers and streams for beaver.

1800s

1820 – The Stephen H. Long expedition makes the first written record of the mountains that will become Rocky, sighted from miles out on the plains. The landmark peak they see on the western horizon is later named for the expedition's leader.

1843 – In September, Rufus B. Sage wanders through what is now Estes Park and writes of "beautiful lateral valleys, intersected by meandering watercourses . . . hemmed in upon the west by vast piles of mountains climbing beyond the clouds . . . ."

1857-1858 – Fur trapper Philip Cranshaw builds the first cabin in the region west of the Continental Divide near Grand Lake.

1859 – In October, Joel Estes and his son Milton follow an old Indian trail into the valley that will bear their name, hunting and prospecting for gold. The family homesteads there in 1860, raising cattle, but leaves in 1866 due to the harsh climate.

1864 – *Rocky Mountain News* founder and editor William Byers and friends stay at the Estes ranch during a failed attempt to summit Longs Peak. Reporting on the adventure, Byers christens the valley "Estes Park."

1868 – Abner Sprague comes to Estes Park.

– John Wesley Powell scouts the headwaters of the Grand (Colorado) River.

– On August 23, Powell, Byers, and L. W. Keplinger make the first recorded ascent of Longs Peak, spending three hours on the summit.

1871 – Addie Alexander becomes the first woman to summit Longs Peak.

1872 – Lord Dunraven arrives in Estes Park on a hunting trip.

1873-1875 – The Hayden Survey photographs, measures, and names many peaks and features in the future Park.

– On September 13, 1873, Ferdinand Hayden, with William Byers and Anna Dickinson, summits Longs Peak.

– Abner and Alberta Sprague homestead in Moraine Park and are among the first to provide food and lodging to guests touring the area.

1876 – Colorado gains statehood.

1877 – Built by Lord Dunraven, the Estes Park Hotel opens as the area's first official hotel.

1879 – Isabella Bird publishes *A Lady's Life in the Rocky Mountains,* detailing her adventures in the future Park.

1880 – The mining camp of Lulu City sprouts along the Colorado River in the Kawuneeche Valley. On the east side, Lord Dunraven has acquired more than 8,000 acres of land in Estes Park.

– The McGraw Ranch is established.

1884 – Enos Mills, age fourteen, arrives in Estes Park to stay with his cousins, Mr. and Mrs. Elkanah Lamb, at their ranch and hotel at the foot of Longs Peak.

1889 – The Larimer County Ditch Company begins building the Grand Ditch to divert water from the Colorado River basin into the Cache la Poudre River to irrigate farms on the Eastern Plains.

1892 – The Kauffman House, a guesthouse for tourists, opens on the shores of Grand Lake.

1900s

1903 – F. O. Stanley arrives in Estes Park. He purchases Lord Dunraven's estate and hotel.

1906 – Local businessmen form the Estes Park Protective and Improvement Association to preserve the area's natural character and promote tourism.

1907 – Enos Mills, James Grafton Rogers, and others begin promoting the idea of creating a national park in the area.

– "Squeaky Bob" Wheeler opens the Hotel de Hardscrabble (later called Phantom Valley Ranch) in the Kawuneeche Valley.

1909 – The 150-room Stanley Hotel opens in Estes Park.

1912 – Twenty-five charter members form the Colorado Mountain Club.

– To replenish the decimated elk population, a herd of forty-nine elk are brought in from Yellowstone and the National Elk Refuge at Jackson Hole.

1913 – The first bill for creating Rocky Mountain National Park is presented to Congress but dies in committee. A second bill fares no better.

– Construction begins on Fall River Road.

1914 – A third bill to create a national park is introduced and is hotly debated.

1915 – January 18, the third bill passes Congress.

– January 26, President Woodrow Wilson signs the bill into law creating Rocky Mountain National Park.

– September 4, 300 dignitaries and citizens brave blustery weather to attend the dedication ceremony for Rocky Mountain National Park.

1916 – Congress authorizes the Organic Act, creating the National Park Service.

– Rocky welcomes a total of 51,000 visitors.

1920 – In September, Fall River Road opens.

1921 – Grand Lake Lodge opens.

– Nearly 280,000 visitors come to Rocky, making it the most popular national park in the country.

1922 – Enos Mills succumbs to blood poisoning from an infected tooth.

1923 – The Holzwarth family opens a large lodge as part of their guest ranch business in the Kawuneeche Valley.

1925 – Ranger Jack Moomaw installs steel cables on the North Face route to the summit of Longs Peak after climber Agnes Vaille dies in a winter ascent of the mountain.

1927 – Funded by Vaille's father, the Agnes Wolcott Vaille Memorial Shelter is constructed at the Keyhole on Longs Peak, providing climbers a modicum of refuge from the elements.

1929 – In October, crews begin construction of Trail Ridge Road.

1930 – The Park Service adds twenty-two square miles of land, including the Never Summer Range, to Rocky.

1931 – In July, with the help of Rocky chief naturalist Dorr Yeager, a group of Estes Park citizens founds the Rocky Mountain Nature Association, one of the country's first national park cooperating organizations.

1932 – Trail Ridge Road opens from the east to Fall River Pass.

– Park naturalist Raymond Gregg launches Rocky's Junior Nature School for children ages seven to sixteen.

1933 – Congress authorizes the Civilian Conservation Corps (CCC). The first CCC workers arrive in Rocky in May.

1935 – Trail Ridge Road opens to through traffic.

– The inaugural edition of *Bob Flame, Rocky Mountain Ranger,* penned by Dorr Yeager, goes on sale.

1936 – Visitation to Rocky hits 550,496.

1937 – The renovated recreation hall of the defunct Moraine Lodge reopens as the Moraine Park Museum.

1939 – On June 23, construction begins on the thirteen-mile Adams Tunnel beneath Rocky.

– Rocky begins to charge an entrance fee. The cost of an annual pass is $1 per car.

1943 – Wartime hardships see Rocky's visitation drop to 130,188.

1947 – On June 23, eight years to the day construction began, the Adams Tunnel is opened, delivering water beneath the Continental Divide to Eastern Slope towns and farms.

1948 – Visitation to Rocky surpasses 1 million for the first time.

1955 – Hidden Valley Winter Use Area opens, featuring two T-bar lifts and a ski lodge.

1956 – The Park expands along its eastern boundary with the addition of 320 acres.

1960 – As part of Mission 66, a new bridge over the Big Thompson River opens, linking Bear Lake Road to Trail Ridge Road, with a new Park entrance at Beaver Meadows.

　– Two climbers from California make the first ascent of The Diamond on Longs Peak's East Face.

1964 – Congress passes the Wilderness Act. Eventually, 249,339 acres within Rocky are designated as wilderness.

1965 – Alpine Visitor Center opens on Fall River Pass as Rocky's first true visitor center.

1967 – Beaver Meadows Visitor Center opens.

1968 – Kawuneeche Visitor Center opens.

　– Visitation to the Park tops 2 million a year.

1970 – The National Park Service launches the Volunteers In Parks (VIP) program nationwide.

1973 – The Park Service removes the cables on the North Face of Longs Peak.

1976 – On July 31, an intense thunderstorm stalls over the upper Big Thompson River, dumping a foot of rain in less than four hours. Floodwaters surge downstream from the Park, causing severe damage in Big Thompson Canyon and killing 143 people.

1978 – Park visitation surpasses 3 million visitors a year. Rocky institutes a free shuttle service to relieve congestion on Bear Lake Road.

　– The Ouzel Lake Fire burns 1,050 acres within the Park, threatening the town of Allenspark.

1982 – At 6 a.m. on July 15, an earthen dam fails and Lawn Lake drains in a minute. The flood surges downstream, killing three people and then overwhelming Cascade Dam. The water floods the town of Estes Park, causing $31 million in damage.

1986 – The headwaters of the Cache la Poudre River within Rocky are designated a National Wild and Scenic River.

1991 – Hidden Valley facilities close.

1996 – Trail Ridge Road is named an All American Road and State Scenic Byway.

2000s and Beyond

2000 – Funded by the Rocky Mountain Nature Association, Fall River Visitor Center opens, housing wildlife exhibits, a discovery room, and a bookstore.

　– Rocky is designated a Globally Important Bird Area by the National Audubon Society.

2001 – The Beaver Meadows Visitor Center is designated a National Historic Landmark.

2003 – A section of the Grand Ditch fails, eroding Lulu Creek and leaving a visible scar on the mountainside.

2015 – Rocky celebrates a century as a national park.

2016 – The National Park Service marks 100 years of protecting the country's natural and cultural wonders for public enjoyment and enrichment.

Bibliography

A Lady's Life in the Rocky Mountains, Isabella Bird, Comstock Editions, 1987

America's Switzerland: Estes Park And Rocky Mountain National Park, the Growth Years, James H. Pickering, University Press of Colorado, 2005

Ancient Denvers, Kirk R. Johnson and Robert G. Raynolds

Arapaho Names & Trails: A Report Of A 1914 Pack Trip, Oliver Toll, RMNA, 2003

Birger Sandzén, The American Van Gogh, *Western Art Collector,* November 2008

Colorado Women: A History, Gail M. Beaton, O'Reilly Media, Inc., 2012

Creating Consumers: The Civilian Conservation Corps in Rocky Mountain National Park, Julia Brock, 2005, Master's Thesis, Florida State University

Enos Mills: Rocky Mountain Naturalist, John Stansfield, Filter Press, 2005

Estes Park and Rocky Mountain National Park Then & Now, James H. Pickering, Westcliffe Publishing, 2006

Ethnographic Assessment and Documentation of Rocky Mountain National Park, John A. Brett, Ph.D., Department of Anthropology, University of Colorado at Denver, 2003

From Pittsburgh to the Rocky Mountains: Major Stephen Long's Expedition 1819-1820, Maxine Benson, ed., Fulcrum Publishers, 1988

It Happened in Rocky Mountain National Park, Phyllis Perry, Morris Book Publishing, 2008.

Land Above the Trees: A Guide to American Alpine Tundra, Ann H. Zwinger and Beatrice E. Willard, Perennial Library Harper & Row, Publishers, 1972

Longs Peak: The Story of Colorado's Favorite Fourteener, Dougald MacDonald, Westcliffe Publishers, 2004

Margaret Fuller Boos, DUpedia, University of Denver, Penrose Library (online resource), http://library.du.edu/dupedia/margaret-fuller-boos

Marketing the Mountains: An Environmental History of Tourism in Rocky Mountain National Park, Jerritt James Frank, University of Kansas Ph.D. dissertation, 2008

Messages in Stone: Colorado's Colorful Geology, Vincent Matthews, Ph.D., ed. Colorado Geological Survey, 2003

My Pioneer Life: The Memoirs of Abner E. Sprague, Abner E. Sprague, Rocky Mountain Nature Association, 1999

Native American Oral History and Cultural Interpretation in Rocky Mountain National Park, Sally McBeth, Ph.D. Anthropology, University of Northern Colorado, project report prepared for RMNP

Roadside Geology of Colorado, Halka Chronic, Mountain Press, 2002

Rocky Mountain Mammals, David M. Armstrong, University of Colorado Press, 2008

Rocky Mountain National Park Administrative History 1915-1965, Lloyd K. Musselman, July 1971, U.S. Department of the Interior National Park Service Office of History and Historic Architecture Eastern Service Center, Washington D.C.

Rocky Mountain National Park Historic Places, William B. Butler, 2008

Rocky Mountain National Park: A History, C. W. Buchholtz, Colorado Associated University Press, 1983

Rocky Mountain Rustic, James Lindberg, Patricia Raney, Janet Robertson, and John Gunn, Rocky Mountain Nature Association, 2004

Sculptor in Buckskin: The Autobiography of Alexander Phimister Proctor, 2nd edition, Katharine C. Ebner, ed., University of Oklahoma Press, 2009

Society of Stukely Westcott Descendants of America website, http://old.sswda.org/Archives/TidBits/Legend.htm

The Golden Pioneer: Biography of Joel Estes, The Man Who Discovered Estes Park, Colleen Estes Cassell, Peanut Butter Publishing, 1999

The Guide to Colorado Mammals, Mary Taylor Young, Fulcrum Publishers, 2012

The Magnificent Mountain Women, Janet Robertson, University of Nebraska Press, 1990

The Mission 66 Program at Rocky Mountain National Park: 1947-1973, Maren Thompson Bzdek and Janet Ore, Colorado State University Public Lands History Center, 2010

The Utes of Colorado in the 20th Century, Richard K. Young, University of Oklahoma Press, 1998

This Blue Hollow: Estes Park, The Early Years, 1859-1915, James H. Pickering, University Press of Colorado, 1999

USGS Science For a Changing World Fact Sheet, *Big Thompson Flood, Colorado, Thirty Years Later,* USGS, 2006

Voices of Courage: In Their Own Spirit, Avis Gray, Ann Feucht, Ryan Gray, self-published, 2002

Women and Nature: Saving the "Wild" West, Glenda Riley, University of Nebraska Press, 1999

Southern Ute Tribe website, www.southern-ute.nsn.us

Index

Page numbers in italic indicate images